THE
BOXING
MISCELLANY

There are many people I wish to dedicate this book to including two men no longer with us, my father, John McDermot White, and my father-in-law, Robert "Bobby" McWilliams.

My sincere thanks also goes to: Paul Miskimmon; Scott McMillan; John Dempsey; Robbie Robinson; Mickey Morrison; Pat O'Neill; Martin Fox; Danny McDonald; Mark Gibson; Sean Harmon; Charlie Sterrett; Frankie Dodds; Damien Friel; Heather Torrens; Adrian and Andrew Abbott; Jim Kyle; Mike Hartley; Bill Clarkson, my mum, Rosaleen White; my brother, David; my sisters, Donna, Michelle and Danielle; my mother-in-law, Ruth McWilliams; and, of course, to my wife, Janice, and our two sons, Marc and Paul.

Thank you one and all.
John

First published in 2009
Second edition published in 2016

Copyright © Carlton Books Limited 2009, 2016

Carlton Books Limited
20 Mortimer Street
London W1T 3JW

A CIP catalogue record for this book is available from the British Library

10 9 8 7 6 5 4 3 2 1

ISBN: 978-1-78097-781-2

Editor: Martin Corteel
Editorial Assistant: David Ballhiemer
Project Art Editor: Luke Griffin
Production: Janette Burgin

Printed in Dubai

JOHN WHITE

THE
BOXING
MISCELLANY

SECOND EDITION

WITH A FOREWORD BY
BARRY MCGUIGAN MBE

CARLTON
BOOKS

⊱ FOREWORD ⊰

I was absolutely delighted when John approached me and asked me to write the foreword to this, his *Boxing Miscellany*. And a word of thanks to John for making a donation to CLIC SARGENT, a charity very close to my heart and indeed close to our family, which is dedicated to helping children with cancer.

Although my dad, Pat, was a famous Irish singer, ever since I can remember all I ever wanted to do when I was growing up in Clones, County Monaghan, was to become a professional boxer. From the moment I placed a pair of boxing gloves on my hands I dedicated myself to the sport and completely immersed myself in my training to be the best fighter I could possibly be. I cannot express in words the love I have for my family for always encouraging me in the sport and for just being there when I need them.

After quickly realizing that boxing was my true vocation in life, I never looked back. I began my professional boxing career on 10 May 1981, beating Selwyn Bell by a knockout in the second round of our bout in Dublin. I then won my next fight, but I was in tears after my third, at the Wembley Arena, when I lost over eight rounds to Peter Eubank, brother of Chris, in a hotly disputed decision. I am happy to say that when I fought Peter a second time I won the fight in eight rounds. My big chance came on 8 June 1985 when I fought Eusebio Pedroza from Panama for his WBA world featherweight title. That magical night at Queens Park Rangers' Loftus Road ground my boyhood dream came true: after winning a unanimous 15-round decision I was a World Champion. The memories from that evening make the hairs on the back of my neck stand out even now and will live with me for ever, as will the tremendous support I always got from my loyal and vociferous fans. I always said that the fans who watched me fight at the King's Hall in Belfast were the greatest fight fans in the world, and I am proud to say I had them in my corner.

The life of a professional boxer can be an arduous one but also a rewarding one. However, it requires a great deal of mental discipline, a steely determination, natural skill and above all else the belief that you can one day be a champion. So to all you young amateur boxers out there, and indeed to all budding sportsmen and sportswomen: "Never ever give up on your dreams, because dreams can come true." When you read John's excellent book you will see what it took for the famous boxing champions of the past and present, including Calzaghe, Chavez, Corbett, De La Hoya, Dempsey, Fitzsimmons, Frazier, Holmes, Jeffries, Johnson, Lewis, Liston, Marciano, Ortiz, Patterson, Tunney and Tyson to name only a few, and not forgetting the greatest of them all, the magnificent Muhammad Ali, to get to the top of their chosen profession.

Enjoy the book, it's a knockout!

Barry McGuigan, MBE

∞ INTRODUCTION ∞

"I am the Greatest, I said that even before I knew I was." Those were the words of Muhammad Ali, the man who brought my attention to boxing. I will never forget watching my first boxing contest, the "Fight of the Century" between Ali and Joe Frazier on 8 March 1971 at Madison Square Garden, New York. There was relentless TV and newspaper build-up to the fight, a bout between two undefeated fighters, both of whom had a legitimate claim to be called the world's best boxer. Ali was the challenger, as Smokin' Joe held boxing's most coveted title, the heavyweight crown. I sat in front of our black & white television set at home and watched in awe as the two men went toe-to-toe, justifying the pre-fight hype. Frazier floored Ali in the final round and retained his belt by a unanimous decision. It was "The Greatest's" first professional loss.

Many other classic fights followed, including Barry McGuigan beating Eusebio Pedroza at Loftus Road, London on 8 June 1985 to claim the WBA world featherweight title; the epic Roberto Duran/Marvin Hagler/Thomas Hearns/Sugar Ray Leonard world middleweight and welterweight duels; Chris Eubank's fiery contests with Nigel Benn; and Steve Collins' tear-ups with both Benn and Eubank.

It was my late father, John McDermot White, who kindled my interest in boxing, telling me stories about Rocky Marciano and how no other boxer alive was fit to lace Rocky's gloves, let alone to step into the ring with him. My dad spoke about Rocky with an undying admiration for his abilities, bravery, raw aggression, skill and talent. There were times when dad told me stories about Marciano that I almost started to believe that he was at Rocky's side for each of his 49 professional bouts, all of which he won. Rocky remains boxing's only world heavyweight champion to retire having won every fight of his professional career. I miss my dad's Rocky tributes so very much.

My personal favourite has to be my fellow Irishman, Steve Collins. I will never forget the build-up to "the Celtic Warrior's" first fight against Chris Eubank at Mill Street, Cork in 1995. Steve had Eubank, the undefeated world super-middleweight champion, so spooked that during a pre-fight interview Eubank looked too physically frightened to even step into the ring. He claimed that he was fighting a machine and that Collins had been hypnotized to feel no pain in the bout. Steve took Eubank's title, retained his crown in a rematch and in two fights with Benn. So, in closing, I can only hope that you have as much enjoyment reading my book as I had compiling the entries for it.

Yours in Sport,

John White
Winter 2016

✺ FIGHTING IN THE GARDEN ✺

Any boxing purist, asked to name the most iconic place in the sport's history, will choose Madison Square Garden (MSG), in the heart of Manhattan in New York City. Although most of today's big-money boxing cards take place in the gambling capital of the world, Las Vegas, the Garden is unquestionably the spiritual home of the pugilistic world.

There have been four Madison Square Gardens. The first two were located at the north-east corner of Madison Square (Madison Avenue and 26th Street). The first, a roofless construction built by P. T. Barnum in 1871, opened as "Barnum's Monster Classical and Geological Hippodrome" and was renamed "Gilmore's Garden" in honour of Patrick Gilmore, America's most famous bandmaster of the era, in 1876. On 31 May 1879 Gilmore's Garden was renamed Madison Square Garden by William Henry Vanderbilt and was primarily used for track cycling.

On 15 December 1925, a new 17,000-seater Garden, located at 50th Street and 8th Avenue, opened. It was built by boxing promoter Tex Rickard, and was known as "The House That Tex Built". The New York Americans, a National Hockey League side, used the Garden as their home venue before Rickard founded his own NHL team, The New York Rangers, who also played there. The current MSG opened on 14 February 1968 and is located at 7th Avenue between 31st and 33rd Streets, at the top of Pennsylvania Station.

Often referred to as simply "The Garden", the arena's main claim to fame is boxing, with 23,190 cramming into the arena on 17 January 1941 to watch Fritzie Zivic successfully defend his world welterweight title against Henry Armstrong. The attendance figure for the fight remains a record for any of the four incarnations of MSG. Down the years many other legendary boxers have fought at MSG including John L. Sullivan, Jess Willard, Roberto Duran, Ken Buchanan, James J. Braddock, Jake LaMotta, Sugar Ray Robinson, Joe Louis, Jack Dempsey and Rocky Marciano. Amazingly, MSG also played host to the only indoor fight Jack Dempsey had.

Today the main sports seen at the Garden are basketball and ice hockey. Without question, the most famous fight ever to take place at the Garden was the Muhammad Ali v. Joe Frazier bout on 8 March 1971, their first meeting, which Frazier won by a unanimous decision, and which was dubbed the "Fight of the Century".

✺ MEGA BUCKS KNOCKOUT ✺

Mike Tyson earned approximately $12 million for his 91-second knockout of Michael Spinks in June 1988, or roughly $132,000 per second.

❧ BOXER TURNED PROMOTER ☙

Gerry Cooney, the so-called "Great White Hope" of the 1980s, retired from boxing after losing to George Foreman on 15 January 1990 in Atlantic City. Cooney lost the two shots he was given to win a world title but managed to win two Golden Gloves heavyweight championships during his career. Of the 28 professional fights he won, 24 were by way of knockout – nine of them in the opening round. When he hung up his gloves he became a boxing promoter for title bouts featuring Roberto Duran, Hector Comacho and Foreman.

Did You Know That?
Cooney played Mickey the Baker in the 1998 film *Mob Queen* and is mentioned in the Samuel L. Jackson movie *The Great White Hype*. He is also mentioned in underground rap duo Zion I's song "Inner Light".

❧ TYSON NOT GOOD ENOUGH ☙

Amazingly, the selection committee did not think Mike Tyson good enough for a place in the USA's boxing team for the 1984 Olympic Games in Los Angeles.

❧ FRAZIER THE UNDERSTUDY ☙

Joe Frazier only made the US boxing team for the 1964 Olympic Games in Tokyo, Japan, as a replacement for the injured Buster Mathis who had to withdraw with a broken hand. Frazier then went on to win the heavyweight gold medal.

❧ A HUGE WAISTLINE ☙

Riddick Bowe is the only boxer to have held all four world heavyweight title belts, namely the IBF, WBA, WBC and WBO championships, although not simultaneously.

❧ WHEN LIGHTNING STRUCK ☙

On 2 September 1946, welterweight Al Couture fought Ralph Watton in Lewinston, Maine, USA. As soon as the opening bell was sounded, Couture landed a punch clean on the jaw of his opponent who hit the deck and was counted out after just 10½ seconds. Although the fight took place over 60 years ago, this remains the fastest knockout in boxing history.

❧ FIGHTING TALK (1) ❧

"I am the Greatest – I said that even before I knew I was."
Muhammad Ali

❧ JOE BAKSI ❧

In 1946 Joe Baksi beat the British light-heavyweight champion Freddie Mills (Mills refused to come out for the seventh round) and then defeated Bruce Woodcock, the British heavyweight champion. Bakis broke Woodcock's jaw before the referee stopped the fight in round 7. Following his impressive win over Woodcock, Bakis was offered the chance to fight Joe Louis for the world heavyweight title. However, before he could fight Louis he had to honour a contract to fight the Swedish heavyweight champion Olle Tandberg in Stockholm, Sweden. Baksi went into the bout on the back of six consecutive wins, including five KOs, and was an overwhelming favourite to beat the Swede. To the astonishment of all, including his challenger, Baksi lost the fight by a split decision. After the defeat he decided to take a year off, but returned to the ring in 1947. Now ranked the No. 3 contender for Louis' title, he had to fight Ezzard Charles for the right to challenge Louis for the belt. Charles defeated Baksi by a TKO in round 7, after which his career faded.

❧ ROCCO TURNS ROCKY ❧

Rocky Kansas was born Rocco Tozzo on 21 April 1895 in Buffalo, New York. He turned professional in 1911 but had to wait 14 years before becoming a world champion. On 7 December 1925 he defeated the reigning world lightweight champion, Johnny Goodrich, taking a 15-round decision. Rocky's reign did not last very long, however, as he lost his belt on 3 July 1926 to Sammy Mandell. Kansas ended his professional career with a record of 125 wins (39 KOs), 27 losses, 13 draws and 6 no contests.

Did You Know That?
Like so many other boxers at the time, Kansas lost all of his savings following the 1929 Wall Street Crash.

❧ WHEN JOE RULED THE GARDEN ❧

Legendary heavyweight champion Joe Louis was undefeated in all eight of his bouts at Madison Square Garden, New York.

❦ THE BOXER WHO WON AN OSCAR ❧

In 1992 Jack Palance (born Volodymyr Palahniuk), veteran of many western films including *Shane* (1953), finally won an Oscar for Best Supporting Actor for his performance as cowboy Curly Washburn in the 1991 comedy *City Slickers*. However, before becoming a Hollywood actor Palance earned a living as a professional boxer during the 1930s, fighting under the name "Jack Brazzo". He won his first 15 fights (12 KOs) before losing a close decision to the future world heavyweight championship contender Joe Baksi. His boxing career was ended by the outbreak of the Second World War, in which he served in the United States Air Force. After the war ended he graduated from Stanford University in 1947 with a BA in Drama and pursued a career on the silver screen.

❦ TYSON'S UPS AND DOWNS ❧

In addition to being the youngest man ever to win the world heavyweight championship Mike Tyson was also the youngest man to lose the title.

❦ THE DANCING DESTROYER ❧

British boxer Herbie Hide (born Herbert Okechukwu Maduagwu in Nigeria), who was nicknamed the "Dancing Destroyer", was the WBO world heavyweight champion from 19 March 1994 to 11 March 1995 and again from 28 June 1997 to 26 June 1999.

❦ TWO BEATINGS ON THE SAME NIGHT ❧

In 1982 Frank Bruno knocked out Zaire's Ali Lukusa in the second round of their bout at West Berlin's Sportshalle. Following the fight Lukusa decided to take a walk in the city but was attacked by several men who beat him up and robbed him.

❦ WYATT EARP TAKES TO THE RING ❧

In 1896, when Bob Fitzsimmons fought Tom Sharkey in San Francisco for the world heavyweight title, Fitzsimmons knocked Sharkey out. However, the referee, the legendary Sheriff Wyatt Earp, ruled that the Fitzsimmons punch was below the belt – although it was seen quite clearly to land above Sharkey's belt – and handed the fight to Sharkey.

A CENTURY OF FIGHTS – 1900–09

6 Apr 00   James J. Jeffries fought Jack Finnegan in Detroit in the first world heavyweight title fight of the decade. The 235lb champion only threw four punches in the fight, all of them landing on the 185lb Finnegan to send him crashing to the canvas. When the fourth punch landed the fight was over in 55 seconds, making it the quickest KO in a heavyweight title fight during the twentieth century.

18 Dec 01   Joe Walcott (the fighter Jersey Joe Walcott was named after) knocked out Rube Ferns in round 5 of their world welterweight title fight at the International Athletic Club, Fort Erie, Ontario, Canada.

25 Jul 02   James J. Jeffries knocked out challenger Bob Fitzsimmons in round 8 of their fight in San Francisco to retain his world heavyweight title.

3 Feb 03   Jack Johnson beat Ed Martin in a gruelling 20-round contest in Los Angeles to claim the "Negro Heavyweight" title.

1 Feb 04   Abe Attell knocked out Harry Forges in the fifth round of their world featherweight title bout in St Louis to retain his belt.

20 Dec 05   Jack O'Brien stopped Bob Fitzsimmons in 14 rounds in San Francisco to win the world light-heavyweight title.

3 Sep 06   Joe Gans beat Battling Nelson on a foul over 42 rounds of boxing in Goldfield, Nevada, to regain the world lightweight title. The bout marked Tex Rickard's promotional debut.

2 Sep 07   In one of the greatest fights of all time Stanley Ketchel, who was sent crashing to the canvas by Joe Thomas in the 27th round, went on to floor his opponent three times before knocking Thomas out in round 32 of their epic middleweight battle in Colma, California. Ketchel ended his career with a record of 52 wins (49 KOs), 4 losses, 4 draws and 4 no decisions.   .

1 Jan 08   In one of the greatest ever battles in the history of the featherweight division, Abe Attell defended his title in a 25-round draw with Owen Moran in Colma, California.

19 Jun 09   Monte Attell knocked out Frankie Neil in the 18th round in Colma, California, to win the vacant bantamweight title.

⚞ MUHAMMAD ALI ⚟

Muhammad Ali was born Cassius Marcellus Clay Jr. on 17 January 1942 in Louisville, Kentucky. Clay took up boxing at the age of 12, encouraged to do so, the story goes, by a Louisville police officer named Joe E. Martin, as a way of channelling his anger over the theft of his bike. Mentored by Martin and trained by Fred Stoner at his nearby gym, Clay became a successful amateur boxer, winning numerous titles as a teenager. However, his greatest achievement as an amateur came at the 1960 Olympic Games in Rome, where he won a gold medal in the light-heavyweight division.

Clay then turned professional and by the end of 1963 Clay had a record of 19–0, with 15 wins by way of KO. Around this time his association with trainer Angelo Dundee came about, and the pair plotted a campaign of world domination. Soon he had claimed some notable scalps, including that of Henry Cooper, and become the No. 1 contender for Sonny Liston's world heavyweight title.

On 25 February 1964, Clay defeated Liston in Miami, Florida, when Liston failed to come out for round 7 of their title bout, and Clay was the new world heavyweight champion. It was during the weigh-in for his shot at Liston's belt that Clay first famously said he would "float like a butterfly and sting like a bee". In the subsequent re-match in May 1965 Ali, as he was now known, having joined the Nation of Islam, knocked Liston out in the opening round.

In April 1967, he was stripped of the world title he had successfully defended nine times and banned from boxing for refusing to fight in the Vietnam War. In October 1970, after the ban was lifted, he stopped Jerry Quarry in three rounds, defeated Oscar Bonavena and earned a shot at Joe Frazier's heavyweight crown. Ali and Frazier, both undefeated, met on 8 March 1971, with Frazier retaining his title by a unanimous decision.

Ali regained the title by beating George Foreman in the "Rumble in the Jungle" on 30 October 1974. A string of successful title defences followed, including a third fight with Frazier dubbed the "Thriller in Manila", when Ali won on a 14th-round stoppage. Ali finally lost his belt to Leon Spinks in February 1978, but proceeded to win it for an unprecedented third time in a September re-match. In June 1979, Ali retired aged 37. However, he returned to boxing in 1980 and was well beaten by the world champion Larry Holmes before losing his last ever bout on points to Trevor Berbick.

Did You Know That?
Ali had a professional record of 56 wins (37 KOs) and 5 defeats.

∾ SMOKIN' JOE'S FIRE GOES OUT ∾

On 15 June 1976, Joe Frazier's boxing career effectively came to an end when George Foreman knocked him out in the fifth round of their NABF heavyweight title bout in Uniondale, New York. It was the fourth loss of Smokin' Joe's career – two to Foreman and two to Muhammad Ali. After this second loss to Foreman, Frazier announced his retirement from boxing. However, five years later, on 3 December 1981, Frazier came out of retirement and drew with Floyd Cummings in Chicago, Illinois.

∾ SUGAR RAY'S HIGH FIVE ∾

The legendary Sugar Ray Robinson won the world middleweight championship for an unprecedented fifth time when he defeated the reigning world champion, Carmen Basilio, on a 15-round split decision in Chicago, Illinois, on 25 May 1958.

∾ THE 33-DAYS WORLD CHAMPION ∾

On 21 May 1933 Tony Canzoneri defeated the reigning world junior-welterweight champion Battling Shaw to reclaim the belt he previously held from 24 April 1931 to 18 January 1932. However, just 33 days after reclaiming the belt, Canzoneri lost it again to Barney Ross – after the shortest reign by any world title-holder in boxing history. Canzoneri is a member of an exclusive group of boxers who won titles at three or more different weights. On 10 February 1928, he won the NBA featherweight belt, defeating Benny Bass in a 15-round decision; on 14 November 1930 he won the world lightweight championship after knocking out the reigning champion Al Singer in the first round; on 24 April 1931 he put his lightweight belt up against Jack "Kid" Berg's world junior-welterweight championship belt and knocked Berg out in round 3 to claim his third different division belt. Canzoneri's defeat of Berg meant that he is one of only three champions in the history of boxing, along with Henry Armstrong and Barney Ross, to hold world titles at two or more different weights *at the same time*. (On 7 November 1988, Sugar Ray Leonard won both the vacant world super-middleweight title and the world light-heavyweight belt after beating Danny Lalonde, but was only permitted to keep one of them. He chose the super-middleweight belt.) Canzoneri ended his professional career with a record of 141 wins (44 KOs), 24 losses, 10 draws and 3 no decisions.

⚜ 20TH-CENTURY TOP 10 HEAVYWEIGHTS ⚜

Rank	Boxer	Record (W–L–D)	KOs	Career
1.	Muhammad Ali	56–5	37	1960–81
2.	Joe Louis	68–3	54	1934–51
3.	Rocky Marciano	49–0	43	1947–55
4.	Jack Dempsey	61–6–8, 6 ND	50	1914–27
=5.	Jack Johnson	78–13–11, 18 ND	49	1897–1938
=5.	Larry Holmes	67–6	43	1973–99
7.	Sonny Liston	50–4	39	1953–70
8.	Joe Frazier	32–4–1	27	1965–81
=9.	Sam Langford	167–38–37, 48 ND	117	1902–26
=9.	Jersey Joe Walcott	53–18–1	33	1930–53

Source: Associated Press, 30 December 1999

⚜ SCOTLAND'S FIRST WORLD CHAMPION ⚜

Benny Lynch, Scotland's first boxing world champion, learned how to box in the carnival booths around the west of Scotland. On 16 May 1934, he won the Scottish flyweight title in Glasgow following a 15-round decision against Jim Campbell. On 9 September 1935, he travelled south from his home in Glasgow and fought and defeated Jackie Brown (TKO in round 2) for the British, European and world flyweight titles at Belle Vue, Manchester. Many American boxing writers believed that Small Montana from the Philippines was the best flyweight in the world, and so the pair met in the ring at Wembley Arena, London, on 9 January 1937 for a unification title bout. Lynch settled the dispute, winning on points over 15 battling rounds. Sadly, alcohol brought a premature end to Benny's boxing career when he was just 25 years old and contributed to his death, from malnutrition, in 1946, at the age of 33. He ended his professional career with a record of 77 wins (15 KOs), 10 losses and 15 draws. *Ring Magazine* named Lynch as the greatest ever Scottish boxer, and in 1998 he was inducted into the International Boxing Hall of Fame. In 2003 his life was made into a film starring Robert Carlyle as Benny.

⚜ WHEN SUGAR RAY MET ROCKY ⚜

In 2005 Sylvester Stallone, who played Rocky Balboa in all six of his Rocky movies, hosted the reality TV programme *The Contender*, which saw 16 young boxing hopefuls given challenges and the task of fighting each other to become The Contender and win $1 million. The popular show co-starred the legendary boxer Sugar Ray Leonard.

⊗ SERVO ACED ⊗

On 29 July 1941 Freddie "Red" Cochrane beat the reigning world welterweight champion, Fritzie Zivic, to claim the belt. Although he held the title for almost five years he never successfully defended it. He had not yet fought when the USA entered the Second World War, and then he was called up for the US armed forces. On 1 February 1946, he put his belt up against Marty Servo (born Mario Severino) and was knocked out in the fourth round. After Servo was crowned world champion he agreed to fight Rocky Graziano in a non-title bout on 29 March 1946 in New York. The "Raging Bull" knocked Servo out and injured his nose so badly that Servo was forced to announce his retirement the next day. He vacated his belt, which was then won by Sugar Ray Robinson, and ended his professional career with a record of 48 wins (15 KOs), 4 losses and 2 draws (his record includes a one-fight comeback in which he was KO'd).

⊗ I'M NOT HEAVY ANYMORE ⊗

Norvel LaFollette Ray Lee represented the USA at the 1952 Olympic Games at Helsinki in boxing's light-heavyweight division. Lee was actually a heavyweight and went to Finland as a reserve but was told he could fight in the lower division if he could make the weight. Lee lost 12lbs and claimed the gold medal after defeating Argentina's Antonio Pacenza in the final. In addition to his gold medal, Lee, born in Eagle Rock, Virginia, on 22 September 1924, was awarded the Val Barker Trophy as the outstanding boxer at the Games.

⊗ WHEN THE GREATEST FELT HUMBLE ⊗

In October 1975, Muhammad Ali fought Joe Frazier for a third time in a Don King promotion dubbed "The Thriller in Manila". Going into the bout Ali clearly thought that Smokin' Joe was well past his best, and he goaded the former world heavyweight champion in the pre-fight press conference, saying: "It will be a killa ... and a chilla ... and a thrilla ... when I get the gorilla in Manila." Frazier was enraged and fought one of the best fights of his life before succumbing to Ali's punches and the sweltering heat, unable to answer the bell for round 15. In fact it was Frazier's trainer, Eddie Futch, who refused to allow his man to continue. After the fight Ali knew he had been involved in one of the toughest battles of his entire career and graciously paid tribute to Frazier. "It was the closest thing to death that I could feel," said Ali.

◎ THE FAB FOUR ◎

Down the years boxing has witnessed several unforgettable series of fights between boxers including Rocky Graziano's trilogy of bouts with Tony Zale for the world middleweight championship, Vincente Saldivar's three wins over Howard Winstone at featherweight, Sugar Ray Robinson's six middleweight meetings with Jake LaMotta (Robinson winning 5–1), the trilogy of bantamweight bouts between Jesus Castillo Aguillera and Ruben Olivares and of course the Muhammad Ali versus Joe Frazier trilogy. However, there is no question that among the most entertaining, controversial and dramatic contests in the history of boxing was the exhilarating eight-fight series produced by four boxers in the welterweight and middleweight divisions during the 1980s. The talented quartet of greats were: Roberto "Hands of Stone" Duran, Marvelous Marvin Hagler, Thomas "Hitman" Hearns and Sugar Ray Leonard. They met a total of eight times and produced some of the greatest rounds and fights in boxing history, most of which took place in Las Vegas (*see* pages 33, 46, 64, 80, 95, 112, 128 and 144).

◎ FIGHTING TALK (2) ◎

"I hated every minute of training, but I said, 'Don't quit. Suffer now and live the rest of your life as a champion'."
Muhammad Ali

◎ PRINCE OF WALES DETHRONED ◎

On 8 March 2008, Enzo Maccarinelli of Wales met England's David Haye in an all-British world cruiserweight championship unification bout at the O2 Arena, London. Maccarinelli, the WBO champion, was blasted to defeat after just five minutes and four seconds of boxing. The winner called his final punch the "Haye-Maker".

◎ CALL THE JUDGE ◎

The world welterweight title fight between Jack Britton and Ted "Kid" Lewis at the Boston Athletic Club on 28 September 1915 is believed to be the first world title fight in the USA in which judges were used. Lewis outpointed Britton over 12 rounds to retain the belt he took from Britton exactly four weeks earlier at the same venue (he also won that fight on points over 12 rounds). Dan Lane refereed the bout and the judges were Bill Hamilton and S.S. Sprago.

✂ HOWARD'S WAY ✂

Kevin Howard caused a sensational shock in the ring in Worcester, Massachusetts, on 11 May 1984 when he sent Sugar Ray Leonard to the floor for the first time in his professional career. However, Leonard got to his feet, stopped Howard in nine rounds and afterwards announced his retirement from boxing.

✂ CRUISING TO VICTORY ✂

Dwight Muhammad Qawi stopped Piet Crous in 11 rounds in Sun City, South Africa, on 27 July 1985 to win the WBA world cruiserweight title. Then, on 22 March 1986, Qawi retained his belt when he stopped Leon Spinks in six rounds in Reno, Nevada.

✂ TUCKER BUSTS DOUGLAS ✂

Tony Tucker stopped James "Buster" Douglas in 10 rounds in Las Vegas, Nevada to win the vacant IBF world heavyweight title on 30 May 1987. Just two months later, on 1 August, Mike Tyson beat Tucker in 12 rounds in Las Vegas to unify the heavyweight division.

✂ A PAIR OF GOLDEN BROTHERS ✂

Leon Spinks won the gold medal in the light-heavyweight division at the 1976 Olympic Games in Montreal, Canada, while at the same Olympiad his younger brother, Michael, also won gold in the middleweight division.

✂ KNOCKOUT SPECIALIST ✂

Sam Langford, who fought as a heavyweight between 1902 and 1926 recorded only two fewer knockouts (137) than modern KO kings, George Foreman (81) and Mike Tyson (58) had career fights. Langford often conceded more than 25–30 lbs in weight to his rivals.

✂ A LESS THAN CLOSE SHAVE ✂

On 23 March 1979, Earnie Shavers upset the form book when he knocked Ken Norton to the canvas twice in the opening round of their bout in Las Vegas. Then, before the bell for the end of the first round was sounded, the referee stopped the contest to prevent Norton from taking any further punishment.

✒ WRITING ON THE PAGE ✒

On 9 March 1984, Tim Witherspoon stopped Greg Page in two rounds in Las Vegas, Nevada, to win the vacant WBA world heavyweight title. Then, on 31 August 1984, the new WBA champion lost to Pinklon Thomas in 12 rounds in Las Vegas for the WBC world heavyweight title.

✒ MONEYBAGS DEMPSEY ✒

During his reign as the world heavyweight champion (4 July 1919 – 23 September 1926), Jack Dempsey was only in the ring for 138 minutes. It is estimated that during his time as champion his purses totalled $2,137,000 – or $15,000 per minute.

✒ THE ROCKFORD SHEIK ✒

Sammy Mandell held the world lightweight championship from 3 July 1926 to 17 July 1930. Born Samuel Mandella in Rockford, Illinois, on 5 February 1904, he was nicknamed the "Rockford Sheik" as he looked like Rudolph Valentino. He won the title from Rocky Kansas (on points) and lost it to Al Singer (knocked out in round 1).

✒ PRINCE CHARLES HITS THE CANVAS ✒

Bobby Czyz sent Prince Charles Williams down to the floor in the first and second rounds of their bout in Las Vegas, Nevada, on 29 October 1987 before Williams fought back to stop Czyz in round 9 and win the IBF world light-heavyweight title.

✒ THE BIG ATTRACTION ✒

Oscar De La Hoya has fought in all of the top six non-heavyweight pay-per-view television contests in boxing history. Unfortunately, "The Golden Boy" lost four of the six. The fights were as follows:

Date	Weight	Opponent	Result
5 May 2007	Light-middle	Floyd Mayweather Jr	L 12
6 May 2005	Light-middle	Ricardo Mayorga	W TKO 6
18 Sep 2004	Middle	Bernard Hopkins	L KO 9
13 Sep 2003	Light-middle	Shane Mosley	L 12
14 Sep 2002	Light-middle	Fernando Vargas	W TKO 11
18 Sep 1999	Welter	Felix Trinidad	L 12

☙ *RING MAGAZINE* FIGHT OF THE YEAR ❧

Year	Weight	Winner	Decision	Loser
1945	Middle	Rocky Graziano	KO 10	Freddie Cochrane
1946	Middle	Tony Zale	KO 6	Rocky Graziano
1947	Middle	Rocky Graziano	KO 6	Tony Zale
1948	Middle	Marcel Cerdan	KO 12	Tony Zale
1949	Lt-heavy	Willie Pep	Pts 15	Sandy Saddler
1950	Middle	Jake LaMotta	KO 15	Laurent Dauthuille
1951	Heavy	Joe Walcott	KO 7	Ezzard Charles
1952	Heavy	Rocky Marciano	KO 13	Joe Walcott
1953	Heavy	Rocky Marciano	KO 11	Roland LaStarza
1954	Heavy	Rocky Marciano	KO 8	Ezzard Charles
1955	Welter	Carmen Basilio	KO 12	Tony DeMarco
1956	Welter	Carmen Basilio	KO 9	Johnny Saxton
1957	Middle	Carmen Basilio	Pts 15	Ray Robinson
1958	Middle	Ray Robinson	Pts 15	Carmen Basilio
1959	Middle	Gene Fullmer	KO 14	Carmen Basilio
1960	Heavy	Floyd Patterson	KO 5	Ingemar Johansson
1961	Light	Joe Brown	Pts 15	Dave Charnley
1962	Middle	Joey Giardello	Pts 10	Henry Hank
1963	Heavy	Cassius Clay	Pts 10	Doug Jones
1964	Heavy	Cassius Clay	KO 7	Sonny Liston
1965	Heavy	Floyd Patterson	Pts 12	George Chuvalo
1966	Lt-heavy	Jose Torres	Pts 15	Eddie Cotton
1967	Middle	Nino Benvenuti	Pts 15	Emile Griffith
1968	Lt-heavy	Dick Tiger	Pts 10	Frank DePaula
1969	Heavy	Joe Frazier	KO 7	Jerry Quarry
1970	Middle	Carlos Monzon	KO 12	Nino Benvenuti
1971	Heavy	Joe Frazier	Pts 15	Muhammad Ali
1972	Lt-heavy	Bob Foster	KO 14	Chris Finnegan
1973	Heavy	George Foreman	KO 2	Joe Frazier
1974	Heavy	Muhammad Ali	KO 8	George Foreman
1975	Heavy	Muhammad Ali	KO 14	Joe Frazier
1976	Heavy	George Foreman	KO 5	Ron Lyle
1977	Heavy	Jimmy Young	Pts 12	George Foreman
1978	Heavy	Leon Spinks	Pts 15	Muhammad Ali
1979	Feather	Danny Lopez	KO 15	Mike Ayala
1980	Lt-heavy	Matt Saad Muhammad	KO 14	Yaqui Lopez
1981	Middle	Sugar Ray Leonard	KO 14	Thomas Hearns
1982	Jr-light	Bobby Chacon	Pts 15	Bazooka Limon
1983	Jr-light	Bobby Chacon	Pts 12	Cornelius Boza-Edwards
1984	Middle	Jose Luis Ramirez	KO 4	Edwin Rosario

1985	Middle	Marvin Hagler	KO 3	Thomas Hearns
1986	Feather	Steve Cruz	Pts 15	Barry McGuigan
1987	Middle	Sugar Ray Leonard	Pts 12	Marvin Hagler
1988	Jr-light	Tony Lopez	Pts 12	Rocky Lockridge
1989	Middle	Roberto Duran	Pts 12	Iran Barkley
1990	Lt-welter	Julio Cesar Chavez	KO 12	Meldrick Taylor
1991	Jr-light	Robert Quiroga	Pts 12	Akeem Anifowoshe
1992	Heavy	Riddick Bowe	Pts 12	Evander Holyfield
1993	Lt-fly	Michael Carbajal	KO 7	Humberto Gonzalez
1994	Middle	Jorge Castro	KO 9	John David Jackson
1995	Light	Saman Sorjaturong	KO 7	Humberto Gonzalez
1996	Heavy	Evander Holyfield	KO 11	Mike Tyson
1997	Jr-light	Arturo Gatti	KO 5	Gabriel Ruelas
1998	Light	Ivan Robinson	Pts 10	Arturo Gatti
1999	Bantam	Paulie Ayala	Pts 12	Johnny Tapia
2000	Lt-feather	Erik Morales	Pts 12	Marco Antonio Barrera
2001	Lt-welter	Micky Ward	Pts 10	Emanuel Burton
2002	Lt-welter	Micky Ward	Pts 10	Arturo Gatti
2003	Lt-welter	Arturo Gatti	Pts 10	Micky Ward
2004	Jr-light	Marco Antonio Barrera	Pts 12	Erik Morales
2005	Light	Diego Corrales	KO 10	Jose Luis Castillo
2006	Jr-light	Somsak Sithchatchawal	KO 10	Mahyar Monshipour
2007	Jr-light	Israel Vazquez	TKO 6	Rafael Marquez
2008	Jr-light	Israel Vazquez	Pts 12	Rafael Marquez
2009	Light	Juan Manuel Vazquez	TKO 9	Juan Diaz
2010	Jr Fly	Giovanni Segura	KO 8	Ivan Calderon
2011	Welter	Victor Ortiz	Pts 12	Andre Berto
2012	Welter	Juan Manuel Vazquez	KO 6	Manny Pacquiao
2013	Welter	Timothy Bradley	Pts 12	Ruslan Provodrikov
2014	Jr Welter	Lucas Matthysse	KO 11	John Molina

❧ THE Z BOYS ❧

On 23 April 1977, two undefeated bantamweight champions, Carlos Zarate and Alfonso Zamora, met in a non-title fight in Inglewood, Los Angeles, California. The two Mexican boxers, nicknamed the "Z Boys" by the US press, elected for the non-title fight when the WBA and WBC could not agree terms for the bout. WBC champion Zarate knocked out WBA champion Zamora in the fourth round. Zarate was WBC champion from 8 May 1976 to 3 June 1979 and had a professional record of 66 wins (63 KOs) and 4 losses, while Zamora was WBA champion from 4 March 1975 to 19 November 1977 and had a professional record of 33 wins (32 KOs) and 5 losses.

♟ FIGHTING TALK (3) ♞

"First your legs go. Then you lose your reflexes. Then you lose your friends."
Willie Pep

♟ FISTS OF DYNAMITE ♞

Victor Anthony Toweel, nicknamed "Dynamite", was an undisputed world bantamweight champion and the first South African to hold a world title. Toweel enjoyed a hugely successful career as an amateur, racking up a record of 188 wins (160 KOs) and only 2 defeats. In 1948 he represented South Africa at the Olympic Games in London but was controversially eliminated in his opening bout at bantamweight by Argentina's Arnoldo Pares. Shortly after returning home from London he turned professional, and in his pro debut on 29 January 1949 he defeated Johannes Landmann in round 2 of their bout. He claimed the South African bantamweight title in only his fourth professional fight, after his opponent Jimmy Webster was disqualified in round 3 for excessive holding. The South African featherweight and British Empire bantamweight titles followed, paving the way for a shot at the world bantamweight championship. On 31 May 1950 he defeated the legendary Manuel Ortiz to take the title in what was only his 14th pro bout. In total he fought 13 times as the World Champion, making three successful title defences and winning the other 10 non-title bouts against many of the division's leading contenders. In his first title defence he had his challenger Danny O'Sullivan down 14 times in Johannesburg, South Africa, on 2 December 1950 before knocking him out in the tenth round. The 14 knockdowns is a world record for a world championship title fight. He then defended his belt against Luis Romero (won in 15 rounds) and Peter Keenan (won in 15 rounds) before losing his crown to Jimmy Carruthers on 15 November 1952. In a rematch with the new world champion on 21 March 1953, Toweel was counted out in round 10. Problems with his eyesight forced South Africa's first, and to date only, undisputed world boxing champion, to retire from boxing when he was just 26 years old, with a professional record of 28 wins (14 KOs), 3 losses and 1 draw.

♟ SPEEDY DEMPSEY ♞

A statistician once calculated that Jack Dempsey's 8–10in punches travelled at approximately 135mph.

☙ HE DIDN'T MISS THE TRAIN ❧

In early 1927, Jack Delaney, the reigning world lightweight champion, relinquished his belt in order to concentrate on landing the heavyweight title. Delaney was matched with Jimmy Maloney, with the winner scheduled to fight Gene Tunney for the heavyweight crown. In the lead-up to the Maloney fight, Delaney got drunk on a night out and he threw a punch at a station porter which missed, causing him to break his right hand on the side of a train. However, the somewhat embarrassed Delaney kept the broken hand a secret from his trainer and fought Maloney on 18 February 1927 in New York. Needless to say, Delaney lost the 10-round decision to Maloney. Delaney ended his professional career with a record of 77 wins (44 KOs), 10 losses, 2 draws, 2 no decisions and 2 no contests. In 1996 he was inducted into the International Boxing Hall of Fame.

Did You Know That?
Delaney had an army of adoring female fans who would scream out his name during his fights. They were known as "Delaney's screaming mammies".

☙ THE OLD MASTER ❧

Joe Gans (born Joseph Gaines) was the world lightweight champion from 12 May 1902, when he defeated Frank Erne, to 9 June 1908, when he lost his belt to "the Durable Dane", Battling Nelson. Nicknamed the "Old Master", he turned professional in 1891 and by the time he fought his last bout in 1909 he had knocked out over 100 opponents. His professional record was an impressive 162 wins (106 KOs), 10 losses, 17 draws and 12 no contests.

☙ SPINKS STRIPPED ❧

The WBC proclaimed Ken Norton as their new world heavyweight champion on 29 March 1978. A month earlier, Leon Spinks had defeated Muhammad Ali to take both the WBA and WBC titles, but he refused to honour a clause in a contract with the WBC stipulating that his first title defence would be against their No. 1 contender, Norton. Spinks, instead, opted for a rematch against the former champion, a bout he lost on points. On 8 June 1978, Norton faced Larry Holmes for the WBC title in Las Vegas, and lost a majority points decision over 15 rounds. Holmes held on to the WBC championship belt until relinquishing it in December 1983.

4 Jul 11   Ad Wolgast knocked out Owen Moran in the 13th round in San Francisco to retain his world lightweight title.

4 Jul 12   Jack Johnson stopped "Fireman" Jim Flynn in the ninth round of their contest in Las Vegas, New Mexico, to retain the world heavyweight title.

29 Apr 13   Nineteen-year-old Johnny Dundee caused a major upset when he held the reigning world featherweight champion Johnny Kilbane to a 20-round draw in Vernon, California. Amazingly it was Dundee's 87th fight, and while Kilbane retained his belt for the next 10 years he refused to give Dundee another crack at his crown. In 1921 Dundee became the first universally recognized world junior-lightweight champion in boxing history when his opponent, George KO Chaney, was disqualified in round 5. Two years later he unified the world featherweight championship when he beat France's Eugene Criqui.

18 Dec 14   Lightweights Eddie Moy and Red Watson met in the last ever scheduled 20-round fight in California, with the fight ending in a draw in San Francisco. The fight ended at 11:30 p.m. Half an hour later California's "four-round era" began, in which all fights in the State were restricted to a four-round limit. The new rule lasted for a decade.

5 Apr 15   Jess Willard knocked out Jack Johnson in round 26 of their encounter to win the world heavyweight title. After the fight a bewildered Johnson said he only lost because he took a dive in the fight, but no one in attendance believed him.

13 May 16   Sam Langford knocked out Joe Jeannette in the 10th round of their bout in Syracuse. It was the only knockout of Jeanette's career.

9 Jan 17   Pete Herman beat Kid Williams in 20 rounds in New Orleans to claim the world bantamweight title.

27 Jul 18   Jack Dempsey knocked out Fred Fulton, previously rated as the No. 1 contender for Jess Willard's world heavyweight title, in 18 seconds of their bout in Harrison, New Jersey.

4 Jul 19   Boxing's "Golden Age" arrived when Jack Dempsey floored the world heavyweight champion Jess Willard seven times in the first round, then claimed the title when a badly battered Willard did not leave his stool for round 4 in Toledo.

∾ THE GOLDEN BANTAM ∾

Brazil's Eder Jofre is widely considered to be the greatest bantamweight champion of all time and one of the greatest pound-for-pound fighters in the history of boxing. Jofre, nicknamed *"Galinho de ouro"* (the Golden Bantam), made his professional debut on 23 March 1957 against Raul Lopez, knocking him out in the fifth round. Just over three and a half years later, 18 November 1960, he claimed the WBA world bantamweight championship belt when he knocked out the defending champion, Eloy Sanchez, in round 6 of their fight in Los Angeles, California. After several successful title defences, he beat Katsuyoshi Aoki in Tokyo, Japan, in 1963 and was subsequently recognized by the WBC as their inaugural world champion, thereby becoming the undisputed bantamweight champion of the world. On 18 May 1965, he lost a fight for the first time, and with it both his WBA and WBC belts, a 15-rounds split decision defeat at the hands of Fighting Harada. On 1 June 1966, Jofre lost the rematch in Tokyo by a unanimous decision and decided to retire. Indeed, Harada was the only boxer ever to defeat Jofre during the Brazilian's professional career. However, three years after his second loss to Harada he made a comeback and after 13 wins on the bounce he was given a shot at Jose Legra's WBC world featherweight title on 5 May 1973 in Brasilia. Jofre beat the reigning champion by a unanimous decision after 15 rounds to claim his second world title at a different weight. He was stripped of the belt on 17 June 1974, and Bobby Chacon became the new WBC world featherweight champion. After knocking out Octavio Famoso Gomez in round 6 of their bout on 8 October 1976, Jofre retired for good with a professional record of 72 wins (50 KOs), 2 losses and 4 draws. In 1992 he was inducted into the International Boxing Hall of Fame.

∾ THE GIRLFRIEND'S KO ∾

In November 1883, Ned Donnelly lost to the legendary Charlie Mitchell and soon afterwards he retired from the ring. However, rather than walk away completely from the sport he became a trainer and a fight promoter. One day in 1885 Donnelly left his gym with his girlfriend and they were attacked by a robber. In the ensuing scrap, Donnelly knocked out their assailant, but while they were still waiting for the police to arrive, the robber came to. This time he was knocked out by Donnelly's girlfriend, who smashed him over the head with her shoe.

℘ APPRENTICE TURNED SORCERER ℘

In 1938, a young boxer named Willie Pep was one of the $3-per-day sparring partners of the legendary Manuel Ortiz, who went on to win the world bantamweight title on 7 August 1942 when he beat Lou Salica. Ortiz was champion until 6 January 1947, when he lost his belt to Harold Dade. He reclaimed it from Dade on 11 March 1947, and held on to it until he lost to Vic Toweel on 31 May 1950. Pep turned professional on 10 July 1940 and just over two years later (on 20 November 1942) he won the world featherweight title, defeating the defending champion, Chalky Wright, a unanimous decision over 15 rounds at Madison Square Garden, New York. On 17 July 1944, Pep fought a non-title bout at Braves Field, Boston, Massachusetts, against none other than Manuel Ortiz, the reigning world bantamweight champion. The judges awarded Pep a 10-rounds unanimous points decision over Ortiz. Pep had come a long way since his meagre $3 per day reward for sparring with Ortiz as he collected a purse of $20,000 for beating his former employer.

℘ THE RUMBLE IN WASHINGTON ℘

On 29 October 1991, Riddick Bowe met Elijah Tillery at the Convention Centre in Washington, DC, for the vacant WBC Continental Americas Heavyweight title. Bowe battered Tillery in the opening round and knocked him down eight seconds before the bell. After the bell had sounded to end that round Tillery walked towards Bowe's corner and started taunting him. Bowe smacked Tillery, which then led to a melee in the ring, Tillery kicked out at Bowe and Bowe laid into him with his fists. Then Rock Newman, Bowe's manager, grabbed Tillery and pulled him over the ropes and out of the ring. Before Bowe could jump out of the ring the security personnel moved in quickly and when Tillery returned to the ring the referee disqualified him for "a flagrant kick" and awarded the victory to Bowe. The pair met in a rematch two months later (on 13 December 1991) with Bowe inflicting Tillery's first ever defeat by TKO in the fourth round.

℘ MILLION DOLLAR BABY ℘

The 2004 movie *Million Dollar Baby*, starring and directed by Clint Eastwood, won four Academy Awards, including Best Picture. The film was based on short stories written by F.X. Toole, the pen name of the boxing trainer Jerry Boyd.

◎ MIKE TYSON ◎

Michael Gerard Tyson was born on 30 June 1966 in Brooklyn, New York, and was only two when his father walked out. The young Mike had a tough upbringing on the streets of Brooklyn, often getting involved in fights with boys who made fun of his lisp, and by the time he turned 14 he had had over 30 arrests for various crimes. Bobby Stewart, a former boxer who acted as Mike's counsellor at his juvenile detention centre, introduced him to boxing and, soon recognizing the raw kid's prodigious talent, brought in Cus D'Amato to train and mentor him further. At D'Amato's gym Mike was trained by Kevin Rooney, as well as Teddy Atlas for a while. After Mike's mum died when he was 16, D'Amato became his legal guardian.

During his amateur career Tyson won 24 of his 27 fights, losing the other three. He was overlooked for the USA's Olympic boxing team in 1984, but still had a rewarding year, winning the National Golden Gloves Heavyweight Championship and then turning professional. He made his pro debut on 6 March 1985, knocking out Hector Mercedes in the first round, and went on to knock out 15 more opponents in the opening round en route to winning his first 28 bouts (26 by KO). However, tragedy struck his life when the man he saw as a father figure, D'Amato, died in November 1985.

Tyson was handed his big opportunity on 22 November 1986, when he faced Trevor Berbick for the WBC world heavyweight title. Tyson knocked Berbick out in round 4 to become the youngest world heavyweight champion in history, aged 20 years, 4 months and 22 days. Tyson proceeded to beat James "Bonecrusher" Smith to take the WBA belt and then took Tony Tucker's IBF belt from his waist to become the first heavyweight to hold all three titles simultaneously. After nine successful title defences Tyson was sensationally beaten by James "Buster" Douglas in Tokyo on 11 February 1990. Following the defeat by Douglas, Tyson's life just seemed to take a downward spiral, with his marriage to Robin Givens ending in divorce, the sacking of Rooney, the breaking with his long-time manager Bill Cayton to sign for Don King, a six-year jail term for rape (of which he served three) and the notorious ear-biting incident against Evander Holyfield. Despite his flaws there is no question that the Rooney-trained Tyson was one of the greatest heavyweight boxers of all time, a man with raw power, tremendous speed and a devastating punch. He ended his career with 50 wins (44 KOs), 6 losses and 2 no contests.

Did You Know That?
During his time in prison (1992–5) Tyson converted to Islam.

♟ FIGHTING TALK (4) ♟

"I never cease to amaze myself. And I say this humbly."
Don King

♟ THE COCKY EDITOR ♟

On 4 July 1910, the chief editor of the *San Francisco Bulletin* was so confident that James J. Jeffries would defeat the reigning world heavyweight champion at the time, Jack Johnson, that he ordered the first run of the newspaper to carry the headline "Jeffries knocks out Jack Johnson". Jeffries, the former world heavyweight champion (1899–1905), came out of retirement to fight the champion, declaring: "I am going into this fight for the sole purpose of proving that a white man is better than a Negro." However, the *Bulletin's* editor received one heck of a shock when one of his reporters sent him a telegram from Reno, Nevada, stating that Johnson had retained his title. Embarrassingly, he quickly had to order the scrapping of those papers already printed and a revised edition informing the readers of Johnson's triumph over Jeffries in 15 rounds.

♟ TRAINER ATTACKS THE REFEREE ♟

In the first minute of round 2 of their bout at Manchester's MEN Arena on 28 September 2002, Ricky Hatton sent Stephen Smith to the floor for the second time. Blood was flowing down Smith's cheek and on to the canvas, and it looked almost certain that the referee Mickey Vann was about to stop the fight. Suddenly, Darkie Smith, Stephen Smith's father and trainer, illegally entered the ring and attacked Vann. Smith senior was a former professional boxer who won 9 of his 42 bouts during the late 1960s and early 1970s. Vann, officiating in his 100th World Championship fight, disqualified Smith when the furore died down, and declared Hatton the winner, which meant that Hatton had successfully defended his World Boxing Union light-welterweight title for the seventh time.

♟ THE ONE AND ONLY ♟

On 22 January 1988, Mike Tyson (the WBA, WBC & IBF world heavyweight champion) knocked out the former world heavyweight champion Larry Holmes in the fourth round of their bout in Atlantic City, New Jersey. It was the only knockout loss Holmes suffered in 75 professional bouts.

WHEN MUM CAME TO THE RESCUE

On 9 September 1989, Tony Wilson fought Steve McCarthy at the Guild Hall, Southampton, England in a light-heavyweight bout. In the third round of the fight McCarthy sent Wilson crashing to the canvas, but he somehow managed to get back up on his feet before the referee, Adrian Morgan, counted him out. However, McCarthy knew his opponent was in trouble and laid into him landing blow after blow as he rested helplessly on the ropes. Then to the complete amazement of everyone in attendance, Wilson's mother, Milna Wilson, entered the ring and proceeded to hit her son's aggressor on the head with her high-heeled shoes. Morgan temporarily suspended the bout as the security staff removed the angry mum from the ring and then summoned both fighters to continue boxing. However, a somewhat shocked Wilson refused to fight on and Morgan awarded the bout to McCarthy by a TKO in round 3.

BOXERS V. JOCKEYS

The Boxers v. Jockeys charity football match was an important fixture in Arsenal Football Club's calendar during the 1950s. The idea was the brainchild of boxing referee Sam Russell, who hoped to raise some funds for Sportsman's Aid. Russell selected the Boxers XI, while two Arsenal players, Jimmy Logie and Arthur Shaw, rounded up a Jockeys XI. The inaugural game was played under floodlights at Arsenal Stadium on 2 April 1951 – the first floodlit game ever played there – with the boxers sporting the Arsenal kit and the jockeys wearing the kit of Arsenal's North London rivals, Tottenham Hotspur. Famous boxers who played in the fixture at one time during their careers included Henry Cooper and Brian London. The novel idea lasted until 1960.

BURNS IN A HURRY

On 18 April 1908, Tommy Burns fought Joseph "Jewey" Smith in Paris. It was somewhat of a mismatch, as Burns was the reigning world heavyweight champion, so in order to put on a good show for the French crowd the two fighters came to an agreement to make the fight last. However, as the champion sat on his stool waiting for the bell to start the fifth round, a photographer took a photo of him and the flash from the camera set fire to one of the ring decorations. Burns went into a panic, forgot the deal he made with his opponent, and proceeded to knock him out just seconds into that fifth round.

❧ THE CUBAN MASTER OF DESTRUCTION ❧

At the 1980 Olympic Games in Moscow, Teofilo Stevenson from Cuba became the first boxer to win three consecutive Olympic gold medals as a heavyweight, indeed the only boxer in Olympic history to win the same weight division in three Olympiads. Hungary's Laszlo Papp was the first boxer to win three Olympic gold medals, claiming the middleweight title in London (1948) and the light-middleweight title in Helsinki (1952) and again in Melbourne (1956). The legendary Papp also captured the European middleweight championship in Oslo in 1949 and the European light-middleweight title in Milan in 1951. He scored 55 first-round knockouts as an amateur.

❧ GOING FULL CIRCLE ❧

On 15 February 1923, Roland Todd beat Ted "Kid" Lewis in 20 rounds at London's Royal Albert Hall to win the British, Empire and European middleweight titles. It meant that Lewis's career had come full circle. Prior to the First World War, Sid Burn was an exceptional fighter who hired a very young Lewis to be his sparring partner, and during their numerous practice bouts Burn would taunt and bully Lewis. Later, after Lewis had won the world welterweight title on 31 August 1915 by defeating Jack Britton in Boston, Massachusetts, he in turn hired Burn as his sparring partner. Around the time that Lewis hired Burn, an up-and-coming young boxer named Roland Taylor would also take part in the sparring.

❧ THE SCOTCH WOP ❧

Johnny Dundee (born Giuseppe Curreri) was the boxer who invented the technique known as the "Scotch Wop" and took his boxing nickname from it. Dundee would lean back and bounce his body off the ropes to propel himself at his opponent with force. However, the technique had mixed results for Dundee as sometimes his opponent reacted faster and landed a punch on his chin to knock him out. Dundee was an exceptional fighter who took on all of the great boxers of his era in the featherweight, junior-lightweight and lightweight divisions including world lightweight champions Freddie Welsh and Willie Ritchie. During his professional career he won 194 fights (22 KOs), lost 60, drew 41 and had 35 no contests. In 1921 he won the world junior-lightweight title and then in 1923 he unified the world featherweight championship.

20TH-CENTURY TOP 10 LIGHT-HEAVIES

On 30 December 1999, a five-member panel for the Associated Press selected their top 10 light-heavyweights of the 20th century:

Rank	Boxer	Record (W–L–D)	KOs	Career
1.	Archie Moore	194–26–8	141	1936–63
2.	Billy Conn	63–11–1	14	1934–48
3.	Ezzard Charles	96–25–1	58	1940–59
4.	*Roy Jones Jr.	53–5	39	1989–99
=5.	Jimmy Bivins	86–25–1	31	1940–55
=5.	Bob Foster	56–8–1	46	1961–78
7.	Harold Johnson	76–11	32	1946–71
=8.	Philadelphia Jack O'Brien	100–7–16, 33 ND	46	1901–12
=8.	Tiger Jack Fox	120–18–6	81	1932–50
10.	Maxie Rosenbloom	208–37–22, 22 ND	19	1923–39

* = active in 1999 (career record to 1 June 2009)   Source: Associated Press, 30 December 1999

WHEN THE FAIRYTALE CAME TO AN END

On 29 November 1974, James J. Braddock, a former world heavyweight champion, nicknamed the "Cinderella Man", died aged 68 in North Bergen, New Jersey. Braddock held the world title from 13 June 1935 to 22 June 1937, when he lost his belt to Joe Louis.

CHACON STOPS MARCANO

Bobby Chacon stopped Alfredo Marcano in nine rounds in Los Angeles on 7 September 1974 to win the WBC world featherweight title. However, on 20 June 1975, Ruben Olivares knocked out Chacon in the second round in Inglewood, Los Angeles, to claim Chacon's belt.

A VERY STRANGE DECISION

On 16 March 1971, Henry Cooper laid his European, Commonwealth and British heavyweight titles on the line against challenger Joe Bugner at Wembley Arena, London. The battle between the two English boxers lasted the full 15 rounds, after which, to the amazement of many, including Cooper, referee Harry Gibbs raised Bugner's arm aloft to declare him the new champion. The crowd jeered the decision, and later that evening a stunned Cooper announced his retirement from the sport. "Our 'Enery", as he was affectionately known by the British public, had been the British champion for 12 years, and many believe to this day that he was robbed of his crown.

✦ ROCKY THE WIMP ✦

During the early 1980s, when Sylvester Stallone was training to play Rocky Balboa in *Rocky III*, the actor gave careful consideration to using a real heavyweight boxer to play the part of James "Clubber" Lang. Stallone invited the hard-punching Earnie Shavers, who lost a world heavyweight title fight to Muhammad Ali in 1977, to spar with him. During their first sparring encounter Shavers was reluctant to hit Stallone with anything other than a jab, but after Stallone said to Shavers, "C'mon Earnie, show me something real," Shavers hit him with a punch so hard that Stallone had to leave the ring to be sick in the toilet. Shavers was nicknamed "The Acorn" (in honour of his shaven head) and the "Black Destroyer".

✦ SAD MEMORIES ✦

In 1964 Bob Dylan released a song entitled "Who Killed Davey Moore?" Defending champion Moore suffered a 10th-round TKO defeat in a world featherweight title fight against Sugar Ramos on 21 March 1963 and died of his injuries four days later.

✦ THE LONGEST FIGHT ✦

On 19 October 1856, eleven years before the publication of the Marquess of Queensberry Rules, James Kelly and Jack Smith fought out a titanic bare-knuckle bout that lasted a staggering 6 hours and 15 minutes near Melbourne, Australia (winner unknown).

Did You Know That?
Mike Madden and Bill Hays fought 185 rounds (6 hours and 3 minutes) at Edenbridge, in Kent, England, on 17 July 1849.

✦ IF AT FIRST YOU DON'T SUCCEED ✦

On 7 March 1951, Jersey Joe Walcott had his fourth crack at the world heavyweight championship when he stepped into the ring with the reigning champion, Ezzard Charles, in Detroit, Michigan. However, for the fourth consecutive time Walcott failed, losing to Charles in 15 rounds. Just over four months later, on 18 July 1951, Walcott had his fifth crack at the title when once again Charles put his belt on the line. This time Jersey Joe prevailed, knocking out the champion in round 7 of their bout in Pittsburgh, to become, at 37, the oldest world heavyweight champion to that date.

THE FAB FOUR: LEONARD V. DURAN (1)

Up first was Leonard, the reigning WBC welterweight champion, against Duran, who moved up the weights to challenge Leonard in the hope that he would become the first world lightweight champion to win the welterweight belt since Henry Armstrong in 1934. The fight took place in the Olympic Stadium, Montreal, Canada on 20 June 1980, a familiar setting for Leonard who won his Olympic gold medal at welterweight in the city in 1976. The 29-year-old challenger Duran threw everything he had at the 24-year-old champion and was the more aggressive boxer, which the judges recognized when they awarded him the fight by unanimous decision over 15 rounds of non-stop slugging action.

BLOODIED BUT UNDETERRED

During their world middleweight title fight on 22 November 1969 in Rome, Luis Rodriguez was battering the hometown defending champion Nino Benvenuti so hard that the Italian was bleeding heavily from cuts above both his eyes and from his nose. However, in round 11 of the bout the bloodied champion knocked out his Cuban challenger with a devastating left hook to the jaw to retain his crown.

MAYWEATHER UNDER THE WEATHER

Julio Cesar Chavez stopped Roger Mayweather inside two rounds in Las Vegas, Nevada on 7 July 1985 to retain his WBC world junior-lightweight title.

DANCING TO A NEW TUNE

Jody Berry, a professional boxer during the 1950s, decided he'd had enough of fighting and began a new career as a professional singer in nightclubs. During his singing career he headlined the Coconut Grove in Los Angeles and sang with jazz legend Ella Fitzgerald.

BLINK AND YOU MAY MISS IT

On 6 August 1993, Gerald "G-Man" McClellan put his WBC world middleweight belt on the line against Jay Bell at the Ruben Rodriguez Coliseum, Bayamon, Puerto Rico. The champion knocked out his opponent inside the opening 20 seconds of the bout in what remains the shortest world title fight in the history of the sport.

THE RING'S 80 BEST BOXERS 1922–2002

1. Sugar Ray Robinson
2. Henry Armstrong
3. Muhammad Ali
4. Joe Louis
5. Roberto Duran
6. Willie Pep
7. Harry Greb
8. Benny Leonard
9. Sugar Ray Leonard
10. Pernell Whitaker
11. Carlos Monzon
12. Rocky Marciano
13. Ezzard Charles
14. Archie Moore
15. Sandy Saddler
16. Jack Dempsey
17. Marvin Hagler
18. Julio Cesar Chavez
19. Eder Jofre
20. Alexis Arguello
21. Barney Ross
22. Evander Holyfield
23. Ike Williams
24. Salvador Sanchez
25. George Foreman
26. Kid Gavilian
27. Larry Holmes
28. Mickey Walker
29. Ruben Olivares
30. Gene Tunney
31. Dick Tiger
32. Fighting Harada
33. Emile Griffith
34. Tony Canzoneri
35. Aaron Pryor
36. Pascual Perez
37. Miguel Canto
38. Manuel Ortiz
39. Charley Burley
40. Carmen Basilio
41. Michael Spinks
42. Joe Frazier
43. Khaosai Galaxy
44. Roy Jones Jr.
45. Tiger Flowers
46. Panama Al Brown
47. Kid Chocolate
48. Joe Brown
49. Tommy Loughran
50. Bernard Hopkins
51. Felix Trinidad
52. Jake LaMotta
53. Lennox Lewis
54. Wilfredo Gomez
55. Bob Foster
56. Jose Napoles
57. Billy Conn
58. Jimmy McLarnin
59. Pancho Villa
60. Carlos Ortiz
61. Bob Montgomery
62. Freddie Miller
63. Benny Lynch
64. Beau Jack
65. Azumah Nelson
66. Eusebio Pedroza
67. Thomas Hearns
68. Wilfred Benitez
69. Antonio Cervantes
70. Ricardo Lopez
71. Sonny Liston
72. Mike Tyson
73. Vicente Saldivar
74. Gene Fullmer
75. Oscar De La Hoya
76. Carlos Zarate
77. Marcel Cerdan
78. Flash Elorde
79. Mike McCallum
80. Harold Johnson

Source: Ring Magazine (2002)

ALL OVER TOO SOON

Mark Breland knocked out Seung Soon Lee in the opening round of their fight in Las Vegas, on 4 February 1989, to claim the vacant WBA world welterweight title.

BOOM BOOM AND BUST

On 14 January 1984, Ray "Boom Boom" Mancini stopped Bobby Chacon in three rounds in Reno, Nevada, to retain his WBA world lightweight title. Less than six months later, on 1 June, Mancini lost his belt on a 14th-round stoppage at the hands of Livingstone Bramble in Buffalo, New York.

LA MERAVIGLIOSA

After he retired, Marvelous Marvin Hagler moved with his family to Italy. He frequently returns to the United States, including for the Intenational Boxing Hall of Fame ceremonies, but in his adopted land he has begun a film career. One of his roles was playing a US marine in *Indio*.

A LESSON FROM THE MASTER

Five months before the 1984 Olympic Games, the three-time heavyweight boxing gold medallist (1972, 1976 and 1980), Cuban legend Teofilo Stevenson, outpointed Tyrell Biggs in a USA v. Cuba match. The American learned his lesson, however, and went on to become the first Olympic super-heavyweight gold medallist in Los Angeles, outpointing Italy's Francisco Damiani (4–1) in the final.

THE NUTTY BOXER

On 21 February 1912, Irish heavyweight boxer Matthew P. O. Curran (nicknamed Nutty Curran) fought the 40-year-old former American champion boxer Kid McCoy in Nice, France. During the fight it is claimed that after Curran sent his opponent to the floor McCoy accepted a drink of brandy from a person at ringside. McCoy drank the brandy, got to his feet, and defeated the Irishman in 10 rounds. McCoy was a very tricky boxer and well known for fooling his opponents in the ring. One of his favourite tricks was to pretend that one of his boot laces had come undone and when his opponent looked down to the floor McCoy caught him off guard and knocked him out.

7 Feb 21   In the final fight of their 20-fight series, Jack Britton beat Ted "Kid" Lewis in 15 rounds in New York to retain his world welterweight championship belt.

1 Nov 22   Mickey Walker beat the defending world welterweight champion of the world, Jack Britton, in 15 rounds in New York to win the title.

14 Sep 23   Inside the first 10 seconds of the opening round of their world heavyweight championship fight the defending champion, Jack Dempsey, was knocked down by Luis Firpo. The champ got to his feet and, clearly angered by the humiliating knockdown, floored his challenger seven times in succession in round 1. Each time the challenger got up, and he even had the audacity to knock Dempsey out of the ring before the end of round 1. In the second round, the champ sent Firpo crashing to the canvas twice, the last time for the full count to retain his heavyweight crown.

24 Mar 24   Harry Greb knocked out Fay Kaiser in the 12th round of their world middleweight championship contest in Baltimore to retain his title.

2 Jul 25   The defending world middleweight champion Harry Greb beat the world welterweight champion Mickey Walker in 15 rounds in New York. It is rumoured that sometime later that evening the two boxers staged a rematch in the street outside a Manhattan speakeasy.

23 Sep 26   A crowd of 120,757 spectators paid to see Jack Dempsey defend his world heavyweight title against Gene Tunney in Philadelphia. The champion did not look himself going into the ring and was stunned with a thunderous right to the chin from his challenger in the opening moments of round 1. The fight was a one-sided affair with Tunney out-boxing the champion over 10 rounds to claim the belt.

12 Dec 27   Tommy Loughran unified the world light-heavyweight title by defeating Jimmy Slattery in 15 rounds in New York.

4 Apr 28   Max Schmeling beat Franz Diener in 15 rounds in Berlin to be crowned the new German heavyweight boxing champion.

18 Jul 29   Tommy Loughran beat James J. Braddock in 15 rounds in New York to retain his world light-heavyweight title.

⬥ FIGHTING TALK (5) ⬥

"If you even dream of beating me you'd better wake up and apologize."
Muhammad Ali

⬥ THE HAMMER OF THOR ⬥

Sweden's Ingemar Johansson won the world heavyweight title on 26 June 1959 after beating the reigning champion, Floyd Patterson, in New York. Johansson, a 5–1 outsider going into the contest, spent the first two rounds of the fight on the back foot, but in round 3 he caught the champ bang on the chin to send him to the canvas. When Patterson rose to his feet his legs began to wobble and Johansson mercilessly landed punch after punch on his opponent, sending him back down to the canvas a further six times in the round. The referee, Ruby Goldstein, had seen enough and stopped the contest to save Patterson from further punishment. Johansson called his punch that sent Patterson down the "Hammer of Thor".

⬥ BOXING'S FIRST GOLDEN BOY ⬥

Joey DeJohn, nicknamed the "Golden Boy", began his boxing career in the Golden Gloves competition. In 1947 he fought an amazing 30 bouts and by the end of the following year he had a record of 45–2. In 1949 DeJohn (born Joey Di Gianni) fought Jake LaMotta for the world middleweight title at the New York State Fairgrounds. DeJohn was stopped in round 8 of the bout by the "Raging Bull", who refused to give him a rematch. He ended his professional career with a record of 74 wins, 14 defeats (he was KO'd in 10 of them) and 2 draws. In 1997 he was inducted into the International Boxing Hall of Fame and is considered by many to be the greatest ever middleweight not to be crowned champion.

⬥ BOXER GOES AWOL AT MSG ⬥

The light-heavyweight bout between Johnny Greco and Bobby Ruffin on 17 November 1947 at New York's Madison Square Garden was almost cancelled. The fight was one of many scheduled on the card that night and a bored Ruffin decided to go for a stroll around MSG to pass the time. To his amazement, when he got back inside the arena the PA announcer was informing the crowd that the bout had been cancelled because Ruffin was missing. Despite being on the floor twice, Ruffin managed a draw against Greco.

❦ CUBA'S HONORARY RUSSIAN ❧

In 1972, the legendary Cuban boxer and winner of three Olympic heavyweight gold medals Teofilo Stevenson was made an Honoured Master of Sports of the USSR, one of a select band of foreign athletes to be awarded the title.

Did You Know That?
Cuban boxers were not allowed to turn professional by order of Fidel Castro. During Stevenson's amateur career he won 302 fights and lost just 22.

❦ TRAGIC AFTERMATH ❧

The death of Benny "Kid" Paret following his fight against Emile Griffith left a deep impression on the Virgin Islander. The effects on Griffith's life and career following the fight in March 1962 were the subject of the documentary *Ring of Fire*.

❦ STARTING YOUNG ❧

Mexican welterweight Pipino Cuevas turned professional when he was just 14 years old to help support his family. He was 22 years old when he lost the world title to Thomas Hearns, but he had already held it for four years.

❦ FAMOUS BOXING NICKNAMES (1) ❧

Nickname	Boxer
The Ambling Alp	Primo Carnera
Baby	Joe Mesi
The Baby-faced Assassin	Marco Antonio Barrera
Bearcat	Tom McMahon
Beast from the East	Nikolay Valuev
The Beast	John Mugabi
Big Daddy	Riddick Bowe
The Blade	Iran Barkley
The Body Snatcher	Mike McCallum
The Boilermaker	James J. Jeffries
Bonecrusher	James Smith
The Boogieman	Jesse Ferguson
Boom Boom	Ray Mancini
Boston Tar Baby / Boston Terror	Sam Langford

◎ WHEN MARCIANO KO'D ALI ◎

In 1969 Rocky Marciano and Muhammad Ali were the only undefeated heavyweight champions of the world. Marciano had retired some 13 years earlier, and Ali had been stripped of his world championship and boxing licence in 1967 after refusing to enlist in the US armed forces to fight in Vietnam. Murray Woroner, a radio producer, agreed to pay Ali $10,000 to participate in a fantasy fight against Marciano which would be filmed but fought out based on the calculations produced by a super-computer after each fighter's career records, strengths, weaknesses and fighting styles were converted by the computer into special formulae. The filming began in 1969 in Miami, Florida, with the pair sparring for 70 rounds or more. Marciano lost over 50lbs for the filming and wore a toupee to make him look the way he did in his prime. As the computer's findings would not be determined until some time later, Ali and Marciano played out every possible fight scenario (including knockdowns, knockouts, etc.), thereby allowing the producer to splice together the appropriate footage when the computer results were known. The final outcome was kept secret until the release of the film. Woroner engaged the services of other former heavyweight champions, James J. Braddock, Joe Louis, Max Schmeling, Jack Sharkey and Jersey Joe Walcott, to record commentary for use in the film. On 20 January 1970, the *Super Fight* was screened in 1,500 cinemas across the USA as well as in Canada and Europe on closed-circuit television and took in $5 million in box office sales. The fans witnessed a classic contest which saw Marciano knock out Ali in round 15, as per the computer's findings. After watching himself get beaten by Rocky, Ali acted shocked and, implying that Marciano had only won because of his colour, he declared, tongue in cheek, "That computer was made in Alabama."

◎ JESUS STOPPED IN INGLEWOOD ◎

Ruben Olivares stopped Jesus Pimentel in 11 rounds in Inglewood, California, on 14 December 1971 to retain his world bantamweight title.

◎ IF YOU CAN'T STAND THE HEAT ◎

In 1952 Charlie Hopkins quit during round 2 of his bout with Fred Guerro in Miami, Florida. However, he did not throw in the towel because he had been hurt by his opponent; he quit claiming it was too hot in the ring of the open-air arena.

ᐯ THE MONEY MAN ᐰ

The record 2.15 million pay-per-view purchases for the Oscar De La Hoya v. Floyd Mayweather fight on 5 May 2007 made De La Hoya the biggest pay-per-view attraction in boxing. His 18 pay-per-view events have generated $612 million in domestic television receipts, followed by Mike Tyson ($545 million) and Evander Holyfield ($543 million). In total De La Hoya's fights have sold 12.55 million PPV units.

ᐯ A SCARE FOR ALI ᐰ

Muhammad Ali's first title defence, after his defeat of George Foreman in 1974, was against a journeyman named Chuck Wepner. Few gave Wepner a chance of upsetting the great Ali but, to the amazement of the crowd and the millions watching on television, Wepner knocked down Ali early in the fight and stayed on his feet until he was TKO'd in the last minute of the 15th and final round.

Did You Know That?
Sylvester Stallone was an up-and-coming young actor when Ali fought Wepner. He watched the bout on pay-per-view and it gave him the idea to write *Rocky*, which, of course, became a box-office blockbuster.

ᐯ NO WAY TO TREAT A CHAMPION ᐰ

On 4 November 1974, England's reigning world middleweight champion Alan Minter, put his belt on the line against the dangerous "Marvelous" Marvin Hagler. The champion was quite simply no match for his challenger on the night and was destroyed in three rounds. However, the night will be remembered more for the disgraceful scenes that followed the American's win at Wembley Arena. Many fans in the audience began to throw bottles at the new champion as he huddled in his corner protected by his corner-men. Indeed, it took Hagler some 20 minutes to reach the safety of his dressing-room.

ᐯ THE GRANDADDY OF CHAMPIONS ᐰ

On 5 November 1994, a 45-year-old George Foreman regained the IBF and WBA world heavyweight championship belts by knocking out Michael Moorer in round 10 of their bout in Las Vegas, Nevada. Foreman's victory, coming 20 years after he lost the heavyweight crown to Muhammad Ali, made him the oldest fighter to win a world championship in any weight division.

◎ THE GREATEST EVER NON-CHAMPION ◎

Sam Langford, known as the "Boston Terror" and the "Boston Tar Baby", is widely regarded as the greatest boxer never to win a world championship. His record was 214 wins (138 KOs), 46 losses, 44 draws, 16 no decisions and 3 no contests. Langford fought anyone who would step into the ring with him and was so fearless that he was very often outweighed by 20–50 pounds. However, despite his impressive record at weights ranging from lightweight to middleweight, a world championship eluded him. During his career Langford pulverized a number of the "White Hopes" who were chasing after Jack Johnson's world heavyweight championship crown, including Ed "Gunboat" Smith, Andre Anderson, Bob Devere, Dan "Porky" Flynn, Jim Barry, "Fireman" Jim Flynn, Tony Ross, John "Sandy" Ferguson and Tom "Bearcat" McMahon (in fact he beat several of these fighters many times). On 26 April 1906, Langford got off the floor twice to give Jack Johnson one of the toughest fights of his career.

◎ THE BOY OF A THOUSAND FIGHTS ◎

Between 1905 and 1918, Russian-born Abe "News Boy" Hollandersky competed in 1,309 boxing matches and 387 wrestling bouts.

◎ WHEN ROCKY LANDED ON THE CANVAS ◎

Rocky Marciano was sent to the canvas just twice in his professional career. The first knockdown occurred in his first world championship bout, against Jersey Joe Walcott, the defending world heavyweight champion, in Philadelphia on 23 September 1952. The second occurred against Archie Moore on 21 September 1955 in New York, when he was making the sixth defence of his title. On both occasions Rocky got up and knocked his opponent out (in Rounds 13 and 9 respectively).

◎ UNIFYING THE BIG BOYS ◎

As the 1970s began, two men were officially named as the world heavyweight champion. The WBA recognized Jimmy Ellis as their champion, after the title had been stripped from Muhammad Ali in 1967. Meanwhile, the New York State Athletic Commission (NYAC) officially recognized Joe Frazier as the champion. In February 1970, the world title was unified when Frazier beat Ellis with a fourth-round knockout to become the undisputed world heavyweight champion.

☙ FIGHTING TALK (6) ☙

"When you are as great as I am it is hard to be humble."
Muhammad Ali

☙ THE VAL BARKER TROPHY ☙

The Val Barker Trophy is presented to the outstanding and most stylish boxer at an Olympic Games. Named in honour of Val Barker, the first Honorary Secretary of the Federation Internationale de Boxe Amateur, it was first awarded at the 1936 Games in Berlin.

Year	Host City	Boxer	Nationality	Weight Division	Medal
1936	Berlin	Louis Laurie	USA	Flyweight	Bronze
1948	London	George Hunter	RSA	Light heavyweight	Gold
1952	Helsinki	Norvel Lee	USA	Light heavyweight	Gold
1956	Melbourne	Dick McTaggart	GBR	Lightweight	Gold
1960	Rome	Giovanni Benvenuti	ITA	Welterweight	Gold
1964	Tokyo	Valeri Popenchenko	URS	Middleweight	Gold
1968	Mexico City	Philip Waruinge	KEN	Featherweight	Bronze
1972	Munich	Teofilo Stevenson	CUB	Heavyweight	Gold
1976	Montréal	Howard Davis, Jr.	USA	Lightweight	Gold
1980	Moscow	Patrizio Oliva	ITA	Light welterweight	Gold
1984	Los Angeles	Paul Gonzales	USA	Light flyweight	Gold
1988	Seoul	Roy Jones, Jr.	USA	Light middleweight	Silver
1992	Barcelona	Roberto Balado	CUB	Super heavyweight	Gold
1996	Atlanta	Vassiliy Jirov	KAZ	Light heavyweight	Gold
2000	Sydney	Oleg Saitov	RUS	Welterweight	Gold
2004	Athens	Bakhtiyar Artayev	KAZ	Welterweight	Gold
2008	Beijing	Vasyl Lomachenko	UKR	Featherweight	Gold
2012	London	Serik Sapiyev	KAZ	Welterweight	Gold

☙ NOT SO SAMART ☙

Australia's Jeff Fenech knocked out Samart Payakaroon of Thailand in four rounds in Sydney, Australia, to win the WBC world super-bantamweight title on 8 May 1987. Then, on 7 March 1988, he stopped Victor Callejas in 10 rounds in Sydney to claim the vacant WBC world featherweight title. "The Marrackville Mauler" retired after losing to Philip Holliday in an IBF world lightweight championship fight in 1996, but returned at the age of 44 on 24 June 2008 to take a majority points decision against Azumah Nelson, the Ghanaian being three weeks short of his 50th birthday.

❧ ROCKY MARCIANO ❧

Rocky Marciano was born Rocco Francis Marchegiano on 1 September 1923 in Brockton, Massachusetts. As a boy Rocky enjoyed baseball and football, but when he was drafted into the army in 1943 he took up boxing. Following his discharge at the end of the war he fought as an amateur in 1946, and after an unsuccessful try-out for the Chicago Cubs a disheartened Rocky decided to become a professional boxer. He changed his name to Rocky Marciano when ring announcers found Marchegiano too difficult to pronounce.

By the spring of 1949, after he had knocked out his first 16 opponents, promoters were starting to pay attention. Then, on 26 October 1951, when he had won his first 37 professional bouts, 32 by way of knockout, Marciano went into the ring with Joe Louis, the former world heavyweight champion. Louis was now well past his peak, and after knocking him out in the eighth round, Rocky cried in Louis' dressing-room after the fight, knowing that he had ended the career of a legend. After four more wins Rocky was finally given a shot at the world heavyweight title when he met the reigning champion Jersey Joe Walcott on 23 September 1952 in Philadelphia. Despite being knocked down in the opening round, Marciano went on to claim the belt, knocking the champion out in round 13.

In the first defence of his belt as champion Marciano faced Walcott in a rematch on 15 May 1953 in Chicago and knocked him out in the opening round. He then had two successful defences in New York, knocking out Roland LaStarza, who had never been knocked down before, and beating Ezzard Charles by a unanimous decision over 15 rounds. His fourth title defence was also against Charles, who split Marciano's nose down the middle and it was so bad that his corner-man could not stop the bleeding. In round 8 the bloodied champion knew he had to knock Charles out or lose his belt, and he floored the challenger to retain his title. Marciano defended his title twice more, knocking out Don Cockell in 1955 and then, in his last bout and sixth title defence on 21 September 1955, knocking out Archie Moore in round 9 of their bout at Yankee Stadium, New York. Seven months later, on 27 April 1956, Rocky announced his retirement from boxing at the age of 31 with an unblemished record of 49 wins from 49 fights, with 43 KOs. He remains the only undefeated world heavyweight champion in the history of the sport.

Did You Know That?
On 31 August 1969, the day before his 46th birthday, Rocky died in a plane crash near Des Moines, Iowa.

☙ KHAN'S FIRST TASTE OF DEFEAT ❧

On 6 September 2008 at the M.E.N. Arena in Manchester, Great Britain's Amir Khan was knocked out inside the first minute of his WBO intercontinental lightweight title defence by Colombia's Breidis Prescott. Khan, a silver medallist at the 2004 Olympic Games in Athens in the lightweight division (losing in the final to Mario Kindelan of Cuba), was sent to the canvas for the first time after just 30 seconds when his challenger landed with two thunderous lefts to the champion's jaw in quick succession. The champion got to his feet but was clearly unsteady and Prescott laid into him again. Khan then hit the floor for a second time before being counted out on 54 seconds to save him from further punishment. It was the 21-year-old Khan's first defeat in 19 bouts since turning professional. Going into the bout, Prescott had knocked out 17 of his previous 19 opponents.

☙ THE GREATEST OPENING ROUND ❧

One of the greatest ever middleweight battles took place at Caesar's Palace, Las Vegas, on 15 April 1985 between Marvelous Marvin Hagler and Thomas "Hitman" Hearns. Indeed, their first-round slug-fest was the greatest opening round of a world championship fight in living memory. Despite suffering from a bad cut over his right eye, which was bleeding profusely, Hagler knocked out Hearns in round 3 to retain his world middleweight belt.

☙ A QUAD FOR THE HITMAN ❧

When Thomas "Hitman" Hearns knocked out Juan Roldan in round 4 of their bout in Las Vegas, Nevada, on 29 October 1987 to win the vacant WBC world middleweight title, it gave him his fourth world title in different weight divisions.

☙ BONECRUSHER CRUSHED ❧

On 9 November 1984, the reigning IBF world heavyweight champion Larry Holmes stopped James "Bonecrusher" Smith in 12 rounds in Las Vegas, Nevada to retain his belt. Just over two years later, on 12 December 1986, Smith stopped Tim Witherspoon in the first round in New York to win the WBA world heavyweight title. Mike Tyson then beat Smith in 12 rounds in Las Vegas on 7 March 1987 to unify the WBA and WBC world heavyweight belts.

20TH-CENTURY TOP 10 MIDDLEWEIGHTS

Rank	Boxer	Record (W–L–D)	KOs	Career
1.	Sugar Ray Robinson	175–19–6	109	1940–65
2.	Harry Greb	115–8–3, 179 ND	51	1913–26
3.	Marvelous Marvin Hagler	62–3–2	53	1973–87
4.	Mickey Walker	93–19–4, 46 ND	60	1919–35
5.	Carlos Monzon	87–3–9	59	1963–77
6.	Charley Burley	84–11–2	50	1936–50
7.	Jake LaMotta	83–19–4	30	1941–54
8.	Stanley Ketchel	53–5–5, 1 NC	49	1903–10
9.	Marcel Cerdan	106–4	61	1934–49
10.	Tony Zale	67–18–2	45	1934–48

Source: Associated Press, 30 December 1999

FIRST AND LAST WORLD TITLES

On 9 January 1900 Terry McGovern, the former world bantamweight champion, became the first fighter to win a world championship in the twentieth century. McGovern sent the defending world featherweight champion George Dixon down to the canvas eight times and claimed the title when the champion was unable to come out for the ninth round of their bout in New York. McGovern was also the last boxer to win a world championship belt in the nineteenth century, his bantamweight title.

THE NIGHT OF THE LONG COUNT

On 22 September 1927, Jack Dempsey sent Gene Tunney crashing to the floor in round 7 of their bruising world heavyweight title clash in Chicago. However, defending champion Tunney managed to get back to his feet, thanks mainly to receiving a longer count than the usual 10 seconds when Dempsey failed to retreat to a neutral corner. In the very next round Tunney floored Dempsey and went on to win the 10-round bout. The gate receipts of $2,658,660 set a new Illinois State record.

A CLOSE SHAVE

When Larry Holmes defended his world heavyweight title against Earnie Shavers in 1979, no one gave Shavers much of a chance of victory. However, Shavers sent Holmes crashing to the canvas before the champ got up and TKO'd Shavers in the 11th round.

❦ THE FAB FOUR: LEONARD V. DURAN (2) ❧

Duran and Leonard met in a rematch in New Orleans on 25 November 1980, Leonard bidding to win back the WBC welterweight title that Duran had taken from him in Montreal, Canada, just five months earlier. This was the fight in which Sugar Ray Leonard famously made Roberto Duran quit, supposedly saying *"No mas"* (No more), in round 8. However, Duran maintains to this day that he never uttered the words *"No mas"* during the bout and what he actually said, in Spanish, was "My stomach is hurting too much." The Duran camp claimed that the US press made up the quote to create a sexy headline. However, what did happen was that in the seventh round Leonard began to taunt the champion and, with approximately 20 seconds of the round remaining, Duran turned his back on Leonard, waved his glove in the air and said to the referee Octavio Mevran, *"No boxeo con el payaso"* (I'm not boxing with this clown). The referee then awarded the fight to Leonard by way of a TKO in round 8.

❦ A SAD ENDING TO A BOUT ❧

On 19 July 1978, Britain's Alan Minter stopped Angelo Jacopucci in 12 rounds in Bellaria, Italy, to regain the European middleweight title. Sadly, Jacupucci died three days later from injuries sustained in his fight with Minter.

❦ THE LUCK OF THE MEXICANS ❧

On St Patrick's Day 1990, it was a Mexican who had all the luck in the shape of Julio Cesar Chavez. The Mexican was staring defeat in the face in the 12th and final round of his bout with Meldrick Taylor on 17 March 1990 in Las Vegas, Nevada. Chavez was behind on all of the judges' scorecards, but with just two seconds of the fight remaining he sensationally knocked out Taylor to unify the IBF and WBC world junior-welterweight titles.

❦ BITTEN BUT NOT BEATEN ❧

The most controversial victory at the 1924 Olympics in Paris was Harry Mallin's quarter-final win in the middleweight boxing division. Roger Brousse won a narrow points decision, but Mallin told his corner that he had been bitten by the Frenchman during the fight. Mallin's corner didn't appeal but a Swedish official complained and Brousse was disqualified, setting off a riot by home fans in the stands.

❦ BROWN BOMBER STAMPED ❧

On 22 June 1993, the legendary former world heavyweight champion, Joe Louis, became the first boxer to be honoured on a US postage stamp. Soon after Louis died of a heart attack on 12 April 1981, the US Postal Service began to receive sackloads of letters from all over the USA requesting a postage stamp honouring the "Brown Bomber". Fittingly, the US Postal Service chose the anniversary date of two of Louis' most historic fights to issue a commemorative stamp. On 22 June 1937, Louis took the title from the reigning champion James J. Braddock, and on 22 June 1938, the Brown Bomber defended his title by defeating the then symbol of white supremacy in Nazi Germany, Max Schmeling.

❦ HE AIN'T HEAVY, HE'S MY BROTHER ❧

On 18 July 1981, Michael Spinks beat Eddie Mustafa Muhammad in 15 rounds in Las Vegas, Nevada to win the WBA world light-heavyweight title. It was a second world title for the Spinks family, his older brother Leon famously beating Muhammad Ali on 15 February 1978 to claim the WBA and WBC world heavyweight titles. Then, on 18 March 1983, Spinks beat Dwight Muhammad Qawi in 15 rounds in Atlantic City to unify the world light-heavyweight titles. On 21 September 1985, Michael became the first ever light-heavyweight champion to win the world heavyweight championship when he won a 15-round unanimous decision against the reigning IBF champion, Larry Holmes. Michael's victory against Holmes made Leon and Michael the first pair of brothers ever to be world heavyweight champions (a feat subsequently matched by the Klitschko brothers, Wladimir and Vitali). His win over Holmes was named *Ring Magazine*'s Upset of the Year. In 1987, he was stripped of his IBF belt for refusing to fight their No. 1 challenger, Tony Tucker, electing instead for a more financially lucrative offer to fight Gerry Cooney in a non-title bout. Spinks knocked out Cooney in the fifth round. During his career he also vacated his WBA, WBC and IBF light-heavyweight belts. When he lost in June 1988 to the world heavyweight champion Mike Tyson, who had him down twice before knocking him out in the first round, he decided to retire with a record of 31 wins (21 KOs) and just the one defeat.

Did You Know That?
When Holmes lost to Michael Spinks he was trying to tie Rocky Marciano's record of 49–0 as the world heavyweight champion.

12 Jun 30 Max Schmeling beat Jack Sharkey on a foul in round 4 of their bout in New York to win the vacant world heavyweight championship.

24 Apr 31 Tony Canzoneri knocked out Jack "Kid" Berg in round 3 of their bout in Chicago to retain his world lightweight title and win the world junior-welterweight crown.

24 Mar 32 Billy Petrolle stopped Battling Battalino in the 12th round of their contest in New York. It was the first and only time Battalino was knocked out during his career.

29 Jun 33 Primo Carnera knocked out reigning world heavyweight champion Jack Sharkey in round 6 of their bout in Long Island to win the belt. However, many journalists were of the opinion that Sharkey took a dive.

29 May 34 Barney Ross beat Jimmy McLarnin on a 15-round split decision in Long Island to win the world welterweight championship.

13 Jun 35 James J. Braddock, struggling financially and nicknamed the "Cinderella Man", was chosen to fight Max Baer for the world heavyweight championship at Madison Square Garden, New York. Baer's manager saw Braddock as easy prey for his man, but the 10–1 outsider beat the defending champion in 15 rounds to win the belt.

29 Jun 36 Despite being knocked down in the opening round, Tony Marino staged a remarkable comeback by knocking out Baltazar Sangchili in the 14th round of their battle in New York to win the world bantamweight title.

19 Jan 37 Benny Lynch beat Small Montana in 15 rounds in Glasgow, Scotland, to unify the flyweight title for the first time in 12 years.

21 Jan 38 In the final fight of his career, former world heavyweight champion James J. Braddock earned a 10-round split decision over Tommy Farr in New York.

28 Jun 39 Tony Galento knocked down defending world heavyweight champion Joe Louis in the third round of their title fight in the Bronx, New York. Louis rallied to knock out Galento in round 4.

TIMMMMBERRR!

Rocky Marciano's huge following of fans used to yell "Timmmmberrr!" when Rocky was about to send an opponent to the canvas.

◇ FIGHTING TALK (7) ◇

"If you screw things up in tennis, it's 15–love. If you screw up in boxing, it's your ass."
Randall "Tex" Cobb

◇ LEST WE FORGET ◇

During the 1920s, Frank E. Churchill was one of the first trainers to recruit street fighters from the Philippines to fight professionally in the USA. However, three of the fighters he brought to the States all tragically lost their lives at a very young age as a result of boxing. On 2 July 1921, featherweight Dencio Cabanela fought Bert McCarthy at the West Melbourne Stadium, Melbourne, Australia. McCarthy was battering the 20-year-old Filipino over the first nine rounds before Cabanela rallied to win round 10. McCarthy easily won Rounds 11 and 12, and in round 13 he had Cabanela on the ropes and laid into him with a barrage of hard punches. The referee, sensing all was not well with Cabanela, stepped in and waved McCarthy to a neutral corner. Cabanela complained that his head was hurting and so the referee stopped the fight and awarded the win to McCarthy by way of a TKO in round 13. When Cabanela got to his dressing-room he collapsed and was taken to hospital, where he died the next morning. Pancho Villa, the world flyweight champion from June 1923 to July 1925 (vacated), died in hospital 10 days after fighting Jimmy McLarnin on 4 July 1925 in a non-title fight at Ewing Field, Oakland, California, aged 23. On 20 April 1926, bantamweight Inocencio Moldes died the day after suffering a beating at the hands of Charles "Bud" Taylor in Milwaukee (although the bout ended in a no decision), aged 21.

◇ MOORE'S GREATEST EVER FIGHT ◇

Archie Moore's battle with Yvon Durelle in Montreal on 10 December 1958 is considered by many boxing historians to be not only Moore's finest ever performance in the ring but also one of the greatest fights of all time. Moore laid his world lightweight title on the line, and it looked set to be wrapped round the waist of a new champion when his challenger sent Moore crashing to the floor three times in the opening round. In the fifth Moore once again found himself on the canvas, but being the champion he was he fought back, floored Durelle three times, and then knocked him out in the 11th round.

❧ THE TOP PUNCHERS ❧

In 2003, *Ring Magazine* published a ranking list of those it considered to be the 100 greatest punchers of all time.

1. Joe Louis
2. Sam Langford
3. Jimmy Wilde
4. Archie Moore
5. Sandy Saddler
6. Stanley Ketchell
7. Jack Dempsey
8. Bob Fitzsimmons
9. George Foreman
10. Earnie Shavers
11. Sugar Ray Robinson
12. Ruben Olivares
13. Wilfredo Gomez
14. Rocky Marciano
15. Sonny Liston
16. Mike Tyson
17. Bob Foster
18. Thomas Hearns
19. Khaosai Galaxy
20. Alexis Arguello
21. Carlos Zarate
22. Max Baer
23. Rocky Graziano
24. Matthew Saad Muhammad
25. Julian Jackson
26. Danny Lopez
27. Gerald McClellan
28. Roberto Duran
29. Rodrigo Valdez
30. Felix Trinidad
31. Pipino Cuevas
32. Jim Jefferies
33. Lennox Lewis
34. Bennie Briscoe
35. Marvin Hagler
36. Edwin Rosario
37. Tommy Ryan
38. John Mugabi
39. Joe Frazier
40. Carlos Monzon
41. Tony Zale
42. Michael Spinks
43. Joe Gans
44. Elmer Ray
45. George Godfrey
46. Naseem Hamed
47. Alfonso Zamora
48. David Tua
49. Cleveland Williams
50. Julio Cesar Chavez
51. Tiger Jack Fox
52. Joe Walcott
53. Gerry Cooney
54. Al (Bummy) Davis
55. Max Schmeling
56. Florentino Fernandez
57. Henry Armstrong
58. Bob Satterfield
59. Al Hostak
60. Jesus Pimentel
61. Eugene (Cyclone) Hart
62. Lew Jenkins
63. Harry Wills
64. Tom Sharkey
65. Terry McGovern
66. Jersey Joe Walcott
67. Kostya Tszyu
68. Leotis Martin
69. Buddy Baer
70. Donovan (Razor) Ruddock
71. Jose Luis Ramirez
72. Tommy Gomez
73. Jose Napoles
74. Kid McCoy
75. Antonio Esparragoza
76. Ricardo Moreno
77. Evander Holyfield
78. Ike Williams

79. Luis Firpo	90. Rodolfo Gonzalez
80. Ricardo Lopez	91. Nigel Benn
81. Humberto Gonzalez	92. (Irish) Bob Murphy
82. Bobby Chacon	93. Paul Berlenbach
83. Jock McAvoy	94. Battling Torres
84. Eduardo Lausse	95. Chalky Wright
85. Eder Jofre	96. George (K.O.) Chaney
86. Charley Burley	97. Andy Ganigan
87. Mike McCallum	98. Fred Fulton
88. Salvador Sanchez	99. Ingemar Johansson
89. Roy Jones Jr.	100. Charley White

Source: Ring Magazine (2003)

↶ THE KENTUCKY PLUMBER ↷

On 28 March 1905, Marvin Hart took the decision in a hotly disputed 20-round heavyweight brawl with Jack Johnson in San Francisco. Hart, nicknamed the "Kentucky Plumber" because of his former trade, earned a considerable amount of respect following his win over the future world champion Johnson. At the time the heavyweight champion was James J. Jeffries, and when he announced his retirement on 2 May 1905 he was asked to select two boxers to fight for the title he was vacating. Jeffries chose Hart and the very experienced Jack Root. Root was the favourite to take the title, having previously beaten Hart in November 1902, but on 3 July 1905 in Reno, Nevada, Hart knocked Root out in the 12th round to take the vacant heavyweight belt. Following one successful defence of his belt, Hart lost his title to Tommy Burns from Canada on 23 February 1906 in Los Angeles.

↶ FLOYD'S REVENGE ↷

On 20 June 1960 Floyd Patterson became the first man to regain the world heavyweight championship title when he knocked out Sweden's Ingemar Johansson in the fifth round of their bout to avenge the brutal defeat Johansson had inflicted on Patterson in New York on 26 June 1959 to take the crown.

↶ MERCEDES PRANGED ↷

On 23 March 1985, an 18-year-old Mike Tyson stepped into the ring for his first professional bout. The awesome teenager knocked out Hector Mercedes in the opening round of their mismatch in Albany, New York.

✑ SUGAR RAY ROBINSON LICKED ✑

In April 2006, the legendary six-time world champion Sugar Ray Robinson was immortalized with a commemorative postage stamp. The dedication ceremony took place at Madison Square Garden, New York, during the *Daily News* Golden Gloves Amateur B.

Did You Know That?
Robinson was once described by Muhammad Ali as "the king, the master, my idol", and he was cited as "pound for pound, the greatest boxer of all time" by *Ring Magazine*.

✑ BACK FOR MORE ... AND THEN SOME ✑

On 5 July 1920, Charley White knocked the reigning world lightweight champion, Benny Leonard, out of the ring in the fifth round of their title bout in Benton Harbor, Michigan. The champ climbed back into the ring and knocked out his opponent in the ninth round to retain his belt.

✑ WHEN THE KID FOOLED THE CHAMPION ✑

Tommy Ryan was born Joseph Youngs on 31 March 1870 in Redwood, New York. On 26 July 1894, he won the world welterweight title after defeating Mysterious Billy Smith in 20 rounds in Minneapolis. However, after successfully defending his belt against Nonpareil Jack Dempsey and Smith in a rematch, he lost a non-title bout to Kid McCoy in Maspeth, New York, on 2 March 1896, knocked out in round 15. McCoy had earlier been used by Ryan as one of his sparring partners and suffered many beatings at the hands of his employer, who was not known for being merciful towards those he sparred with. When McCoy found employment elsewhere he swore to get his revenge on his former employer. Legend has it that McCoy enticed Ryan to fight him by arranging a meeting at which he pretended to be unwell. McCoy, known for being a trickster, patted flour on his face before they met and slumped his shoulders to give the champion the impression that he would be up against a very weakened fighter. Ryan duly agreed to fight him, and for the next two weeks McCoy trained non-stop while Ryan did not train as hard as he normally would for a bout. McCoy's ruse had done the trick. Ryan went on to win the world middleweight championship in 1899 – a title he vacated in 1906. When he retired in 1908, Ryan had a professional record of 86 wins (68 KOs), 3 losses and 6 draws.

THE BIONIC MAN

Gerhardus Christian (Gerrie) Coetzee made boxing history twice during his professional career. He was not only the first ever boxer from the continent of Africa to fight for the world heavyweight title, but also later the first to win it and the first white world heavyweight champion for 23 years. He was nicknamed the "Bionic Man" because he always had trouble with his right hand and had several corrective pieces inserted into it over the course of three operations.

Coetzee's first world championship fight – for the title vacated by Muhammad Ali – ended with a 15-round points defeat to John Tate. His second crack at the title was against the man who took it from Tate, Mike Weaver. They met in South Africa, but Coetzee was knocked out by Weaver in round 13. A third world title fight came in Akron, Ohio, against the WBA champion, Michael Dokes. In the 10th round, Coetzee landed a beauty of a right hand square on Dokes's chin, knocking him out, to claim the belt he had coveted for so long. Sadly, he hit Dokes so hard that he broke his right hand, and it was surgically repaired five days later. The Dokes fight was *KO Magazine*'s Upset of the Year for 1983.

Although the boxing public clamoured for a fight against Larry Holmes, the South African defended his title against Greg Page and was knocked out in the eighth round. After a first-round knockout defeat to Britain's Frank Bruno, Coetzee decided to retire. However, he came out of retirement twice during the early 1990s and won several fights before losing to the former world middleweight and light-heavyweight champion, Iran Barkley. After Barkley's 10th-round knockout, Coetzee retired for good. He ended his professional career with a record of 33 wins (20 KOs), 6 losses and a draw.

A UNIQUE CHAMPION

Ken Norton is the only world heavyweight boxing champion never to win a world title fight. He was awarded the WBC belt when Leon Spinks refused to fight him, but lost his first defence to Larry Holmes.

A TOPSY-TURVY YEAR

On 30 January 1982, Wilfred Benitez beat Roberto Duran in 15 rounds in Las Vegas, Nevada, to retain his WBC world junior-middleweight title. At the end of the year, on 3 December, Thomas "Hitman" Hearns beat Benitez in 15 rounds to take his crown.

ROCKY ENDS SERVO'S CAREER

On 29 March 1946, Rocky Graziano knocked out the world welterweight champion Marty Servo in round 2 of their fight in New York. Graziano broke Servo's nose so badly in the fight that a few months later Servo quit boxing.

NOT MUCH TO SING ABOUT

On 17 July 1930, at Yankee Stadium, New York, Al Singer knocked out Sammy Mandell in round 1 to become world lightweight champion. When Tony Canzoneri knocked Singer out in the opening round of their bout at Madison Square Garden, New York, on 14 November 1931, Singer became the first and to date only boxer in history to win and lose a world championship with a first-round knockout. Singer was born in New York City on 6 September 1906 and was killed in a bar fight in the Big Apple, on 20 April 1961.

BIG GEORGE'S FIRST GOODBYE

Jimmy Young stopped George Foreman in the final round of their bout in San Juan, Puerto Rico, en route to a unanimous points decision victory on 17 March 1977. After the fight the former world heavyweight champion Foreman announced his retirement from the sport – well, for 10 years anyway.

WATCH THAT MICROPHONE

Prior to his fight against Jimmy McLarnin in New York on 8 May 1936, Tony Canzoneri banged his head on the microphone which was overhanging the ring and was left dazed. Needless to say, McLarnin took full advantage of his opponent's mishap and battered him in the opening round. However, in round 2 McLarnin was sent crashing to the canvas and Canzoneri took the 10-round decision to win the fight.

MARCIANO EVENTUALLY GETS LICKED

In 1999, the former undefeated world heavyweight boxing champion Rocky Marciano, appeared on a commemorative 33-cents US postage stamp. The image of Rocky portrayed the same image his fans saw in all 49 of his professional fights, the referee raising Rocky's arm in the air to declare him the winner of the bout.

☙ FIGHTING TALK (8) ☜

"A champion is someone who gets up when he can't."
Jack Dempsey

☙ TOO OLD TO FIGHT ☜

On 13 September 1975, Venezuela's Luis Alberto Estaba won WBC world light-flyweight title when he knocked out Rafael Lovera in the fourth round of their contest in Caracas, Venezuela. Estaba, nicknamed "Lumumba" because he looked very similar to the Congolese leader Patrice Lumumba, successfully defended his belt 12 times. Estaba only took up boxing in 1967 when he was 29 years old and fought his last bout on 29 July 1978. Venezuelan boxing laws banned anyone aged 40 years or older from boxing professionally, Estaba celebrated his 40th birthday on 13 August 1978. He lost his title to Freddie Castillo, with a 14th-round TKO on 19 February 1978, and ended his professional career with a record of 41 wins (27 KOs), 9 losses and 2 draws.

☙ STARTING YOUNG ☜

Battling Nelson was born Oscar Mattheus Nielsen in Copenhagen, Denmark, on 8 June 1882, but was brought up in Chicago, Illinois. He was 14 years old when he fought his first professional bout. Challenged to last three rounds in the ring against a fighter in a travelling circus, the young Dane knocked out his opponent in the first round.

☙ JOHNSON AND THE TWO MUHAMMADS ☜

After Matthew Franklin stopped Marvin Johnson in round 8 of their bout in Indianapolis on 22 April 1979 to win the WBC world light-heavyweight title, he changed his name to Matthew Saad Muhammad. The following year, after Eddie Gregory stopped Johnson in 11 rounds in Knoxville, Tennessee, on 31 March 1980 to win the WBA world light-heavyweight title, Gregory changed his name to Eddie Mustafa Muhammad.

Did You Know That?
Dwight Braxton stopped Matthew Saad Muhammad in round 10 in Atlantic City on 19 December 1981 to claim the WBC title – and later changed his name to Dwight Muhammad Qawi.

⚜ THE RAGAMUFFIN MAN ⚜

Britain's Lloyd Honeyghan (born on 22 April 1960 in Jamaica) caused a huge sensation in boxing on 27 September 1986 when he stopped Donald Curry in six rounds in Atlantic City to win the WBA, WBC and IBF world welterweight championships. Before the fight, Curry had dismissed Honeyghan's chances of taking his belt, asking, "Who is this ragamuffin?" Boxing fans loved Honeyghan's no-nonsense, all-out aggressive style of fighting and flocked to see him. After several successful defences of his title, Honeyghan lost the WBC belt to Jorge Vaca on points in 1987, when the fight was stopped owing to a clash of heads resulting in Vaca bleeding profusely. Honeyghan then sensationally threw his WBA belt in a London dustbin as a protest against the WBA's sanctioning of fights in apartheid South Africa. Honeyghan said he would rather vacate the title than defend it against the WBA's No. 1 contender, Harold Volbrecht from South Africa. Not long after Honeyghan relinquished the belt the WBA took the decision to cease sanctioning fights in South Africa. On 6 February 1987, Mark Breland knocked out Volbrecht in round 7 of their bout in Atlantic City to win the WBA belt thrown away by Honeyghan, who was stripped of his IBF belt on 28 October 1987. However, Lloyd then became only the second British boxer in history to regain a world title when he regained the WBC belt, knocking Vaca out in their rematch on 29 March 1988 – the first Briton to achieve the feat was Ted "Kid" Lewis. When he apologized to the WBA for throwing the belt in a bin he was permitted to have another crack at it but lost to Mark Breland in 1990. Honeyghan then began to fight at light-middleweight and won the Commonwealth title at this weight. In 1995, following a defeat by Adrian Dodson, he retired with a professional record of 43 wins (31 KOs) and 5 losses.

⚜ THIS SWEDE DOES THE MASHING ⚜

On 26 June 1959, Swedish challenger Ingemar Johansson pulled off one of boxing's biggest shocks when he knocked heavyweight champion Floyd Patterson to the canvas seven times in round 3 of their bout in Yankee Stadium, New York, to take his world title.

⚜ LEWIS UNIFIES THE HEAVYWEIGHTS ⚜

On 13 November 1999, Lennox Lewis defeated Evander Holyfield over 12 rounds in Las Vegas to unify the world heavyweight division.

ᝪᝪ "MARVELOUS" MARVIN HAGLER ᝪᝪ

Marvin Nathaniel Hagler was born in Newark, New Jersey, on 23 May 1954. The young Hagler was raised by his mother in Newark's Central Ward area, and when he was just 13 years old his family home was destroyed during the Newark Riots of July 1967. The Hagler family then moved to Brockton, Massachusetts, the birthplace of Rocky Marciano. In 1969 the young Marvin visited the Petronelli Brothers' gym and there and then decided he wanted boxing to be his life. Four years later the Petronelli Brothers developed the raw talent Hagler possessed into the 1973 US National AAU Champion at 165lbs.

Hagler then turned professional, but early defeats to Willie Monroe and Bobby "Boogaloo" Watts made it difficult to get a shot at the middleweight title. A frustrated Hagler could only look on with envy as other fighters like Hugo Corro and Carlos Monzon all got their big fight day. Hagler, however, turned his envy into a steely determination which would soon reap untold dividends for the kid from Newark. After he defeated Monroe and Watts in rematches he was signed up by Bob Arum, who got him a crack at the world title in November 1979. His world middleweight title fight with Vito Antuofermo ended in a controversial draw, but the champion then lost his belt to Alan Minter, who offered Hagler a second shot at the title. Hagler destroyed the British favourite at the Wembley Arena and had to be escorted to the dressing-room under a barrage of beer bottles and glasses thrown at him by the disgruntled Minter fans. After he had successfully defended his title on seven occasions (none of the bouts went beyond round 11), the fight all boxing fans wanted to see finally took place on 10 November 1983 when Hagler faced Roberto Duran in Las Vegas. The undisputed champion beat Duran by a unanimous points decision over 15 rounds (the first challenger to last the distance with Hagler in a world championship bout). Having defeated Juan Roldan (the only man to drop him), Hagler fought Thomas "Hitman" Hearns in Las Vegas on 15 April 1985. In a fight billed as "The War" a bloodied champion knocked out Hearns in round 3. After defending his belt against John "The Beast" Mugabi, Hagler fought Sugar Ray Leonard for the WBC world middleweight championship in Las Vegas on 6 April 1987 and lost the bout on a controversial split decision. Following this defeat he decided to retire with a professional record of 62 wins (52 KOs), 3 losses and 2 draws.

Did You Know That?
Bob Arum worked as a lawyer in the White House during John F. Kennedy's reign as the President of the USA.

❡ A MAN FOR ALL WEIGHTS ❡

Len Harvey was born on 11 July 1907 in Stoke Climsland, Cornwall, and amazingly fought at every weight division of his day. The 12-year-old Harvey began his boxing career as a flyweight and by the time he hung up his gloves some 23 years later he was fighting as a heavyweight. In 1926, when he was 18 years old, he fought Harry Mason for Mason's British welterweight title but was held to a draw, meaning the champion retained his belt.

On 16 May 1929, he was given a crack at Alex Ireland's British middleweight title and knocked out the champion in the seventh round to take the belt. Harvey, a proud Englishman, made six successful defences of his title between 1929 and 1933. During this period he also fought France's Marcel Thil for the world middleweight championship but lost a close contest on points. On 10 April 1933, Harvey defended his British middleweight title against Jock McAvoy but lost the bout. Two months later he fought Eddie Phillips for his British light-heavyweight belt and took Phillips's belts on points. Then, on 30 November 1933, Harvey claimed his third British title at a different weight when he defeated the previously unbeaten Jack Petersen to become the new British heavyweight champion.

Following his win over Petersen, Harvey went on to beat Canada's Larry Gains to become the Empire heavyweight champion. However, in a rematch with Petersen, Harvey lost both of his heavyweight belts when he was forced to retire in round 12, suffering badly from cuts. Undeterred, Harvey then went on to fight for the world light-heavyweight title on 9 November 1936, but was beaten on points by John Henry Lewis. After his loss to Lewis, Harvey then regained the British heavyweight title by disqualification against his old adversary, Eddie Phillips.

During the Second World War, Harvey served in the Royal Air Force but continued boxing. On 20 June 1942, he defended his world titles against Freddie Mills at White Hart Lane stadium, the home of Tottenham Hotspur Football Club. However, the 35-year-old champion was knocked out in the second round, only the second time he had been stopped in his professional career and the first time he had been knocked out.

Harvey retired after the fight with a professional record of 111 wins, 13 losses and 9 draws. He died in London on 28 November 1976. In 2008, more than 65 years after his final fight, and more than 30 years after his death, this legendary British fighter was inducted into the International Boxing Hall of Fame.

✍ THE SOFT GIANT ✍

Axel Schulz, the German heavyweight champion known as *"Der weiche Riese"* (the Soft Giant), had three unsuccessful world title shots in the space of just 14 months. On 22 April 1995, he lost a controversial decision on points to the reigning IBF champion George Foreman. When Foreman refused a rematch with Schulz he was stripped of the IBF belt, which led to Schulz fighting Francois Botha for the vacant title on 12 December 1995, Schulz losing by a split decision, but this was later declared a no contest when Botha failed a drugs test. His third chance came on 22 June 1996, when he faced Michael Moorer for the still vacant IBF belt. Schulz lost to Moorer on points.

✍ TWICE HIS AGE ✍

On 30 November 1956, Floyd Patterson, aged 21, knocked out Archie Moore, age 42, in round 5 of their bout in Chicago, Illinois, to claim the vacant world heavyweight title (Rocky Marciano had vacated the belt when he retired undefeated that April). Patterson became the youngest boxer to win the world heavyweight title (later surpassed by Mike Tyson), while Moore became the oldest to fight for it.

✍ HISTORY-MAKING KNOCKOUT ✍

When Sonny Liston knocked out Floyd Patterson just 126 seconds into the first round of their world heavyweight championship fight in Chicago on 25 September 1962, he became the first boxer in history to win the world heavyweight title on a first-round KO. Liston repeated the feat against Patterson on 22 July 1963 in Las Vegas, again knocking him out in the opening round to retain his title. On this occasion Patterson lasted four seconds longer (2:10).

✍ ONE AND DONE ✍

When Rafael Lovera from Paraguay was ordered to take on Venezuela's Luis Alberto Estaba for the vacant WBC world light-flyweight championship in Caracas, Venezuela, on 13 September 1975, he became only the second boxer in history, after Pete Rademacher (who was knocked out by Floyd Patterson in their 1957 heavyweight championship clash), to fight for a world title in his first professional bout. Amazingly, the records seem to suggest that the fourth-round knockout suffered by Lovera was too much for him because he never fought again.

✑ A CENTURY OF FIGHTS – 1940-49 ✑

1 Mar 40   Henry Armstrong fought defending world middleweight champion Ceferino Garcia in Los Angeles seeking his fourth world title. Many at the fight thought Armstrong had done enough to win it, but it was called a draw.

28 Nov 41   Georgie Abrams had Tony Zale down in the opening round of their fight in New York, but Zale got to his feet and beat Abrams in 15 rounds to become the first undisputed world middleweight champion since 1929.

9 Jan 42   Joe Louis knocked out Buddy Baer in the first round of their fight in New York to retain his world heavyweight title.

5 Feb 43   Sugar Ray Robinson faced Jake LaMotta in Detroit looking for his 41st consecutive win as a professional. However, LaMotta shocked Sugar Ray in 10 rounds.

22 Dec 44   After having been saved by the bell following a thunderous right hook from Rocky Graziano, Harold Green recovered his senses and beat Graziano in 10 rounds in New York.

18 Apr 45   Ike Williams met Juan Zurita in Mexico City for the NBA lightweight title. After Williams knocked out the home favourite in the second round, many of the Mexican fighter's fans climbed into the ring to attack the new champion and his team. Williams was forced to leave without being presented with the championship belt.

7 Jun 46   Willie Pep knocked out Sal Bartolo in the 12th round in New York to unify the featherweight title.

17 Mar 47   Rocky Marciano's professional debut ended with a knock-out of Lee Epperson in Holyoke, Massachusetts.

25 Jun 48   Despite being knocked down in the third round of their world heavyweight title fight in New York, the reigning champion, Joe Louis, rallied to knock out Jersey Joe Walcott in the 11th round, his 24th consecutive defence of his belt.

16 Jun 49   Jake LaMotta stopped Marcel Cerdan in the 10th round of their fight in Detroit to win the world middleweight title.

✑ SPIDER-MAN KNOCKED OUT COLD ✑

On 19 September 1932 in Toronto, Canada, the reigning world bantamweight champion, Panama Al Brown, knocked out Emile "Spider" Pladner in the opening round of their bout to retain his belt.

◈ 20TH-CENTURY TOP 10 WELTERWEIGHTS ◈

Rank	Boxer	Record (W–L–D)	KOs	Career
1.	Sugar Ray Robinson	175–19–6	109	1940–65
2.	Henry Armstrong	151–21–9	101	1931–45
3.	Sugar Ray Leonard	36–3–1	25	1977–97
4.	Jose Napoles	77–7	54	1958–77
5.	Barney Ross	72–4–3, 2 ND	22	1929–38
6.	Carmen Basilio	56–16–7	27	1948–61
7.	Mickey Walker	93–19–4, 46 ND	60	1919–35
8.	Emile Griffith	85–24–2	23	1958–77
9.	Kid Gavilan	107–30–6	28	1943–58
10.	Luis Rodriguez	107–13	49	1959–72

Source: Associated Press, 30 December 1999

◈ ONE OF THE BIG THREE ◈

Along with Muhammad Ali and George Foreman, Joe Frazier was one of the greatest heavyweight boxers of the 1970s. Smokin' Joe unified the heavyweight title in 1970 but was knocked out by Big George in January 1973 during their bout in Kingston, Jamaica. During his reign as champion Frazier only defended his title four times. In November 1970 he hammered Bob Foster; in March 1971 he beat Ali in their first meeting; and he defeated Terry Daniels in January 1972 and Ron Stander in May 1972.

◈ GOLDEN GLOVES ◈

The most successful Olympic boxing team to represent the United States is the team that went to the 1976 Games in Montreal. Five of the team returned home with gold medals: Leo Randolph won at flyweight, Howard Davis Jr. at lightweight, Sugar Ray Leonard at light-welterweight, Michael Spinks at middleweight and Leon Spinks at light-heavyweight. All except Davis went on to become professional world champions.

◈ ALI'S RING EXILE ENDS ◈

On 26 October 1970, Muhammad Ali fought his first bout in 3½ years in Atlanta, Georgia, stopping Jerry Quarry on cuts in the third round. The pair met again on 27 June 1972, when Ali stopped Quarry in seven rounds in Las Vegas to retain the NABF heavyweight title which he had won from Jimmy Ellis in Houston on 26 July 1971.

✒ CUBAN RING MASTERS ✒

In the boxing competitions at the 1980 Olympics in Moscow, Cuba won six gold, two silver and two bronze medals from the 11 weight divisions. The only weight division in which they missed out on a podium place was flyweight. This impressive haul equalled the Olympic record which had stood since the St Louis Games in 1904, when the USA won 11 boxing medals on home soil. On that occasion, however, unlike Moscow, there were hardly any fighters from outside the USA.

✒ THE TWENTIETH-CENTURY BOY ✒

On 1 January 1900 Kid McCoy inaugurated boxing in the twentieth century by knocking out Peter Maher in the fifth round of their heavyweight bout in Coney Island. McCoy was a colourful character in and out of the ring, recording 81 wins (55 KOs), 6 losses, 9 no decisions and 6 disqualifications during his professional career. It is alleged that when McCoy went on a boxing tour of Australia and the Pacific Islands during the early 1900s he would agree to fight anyone to boost his income from the tour. McCoy, who fought at welterweight and light-heavyweight during his career, weighed around 160lbs on the tour and once agreed to fight a massive local native boxer weighing in excess of 250lbs. In the lead-up to the bout McCoy decided to carry out a spying mission on his forthcoming opponent and noticed that he fought barefoot. When the bell sounded for the fight the next day, McCoy's corner-man threw a handful of brass tacks into the ring which were stepped on by both men. When his challenger felt the pain of the tacks piercing his foot he hopped around on one foot, and as he did so McCoy knocked him out. During the early years of the movie industry in the early twentieth century, McCoy appeared in several movies and was very friendly with Charlie Chaplin. Legend has it that the term "the Real McCoy" refers him and was coined by a bar-room bully who challenged McCoy to a fight, not knowing McCoy was a professional boxer. The man was knocked out, and on coming round supposedly said: "Now that was the real McCoy."

Did You Know That?
McCoy was convicted of murdering Mrs Mors, a divorcee with whom he had a relationship at the time of her death on 12 August 1924. Sent to San Quentin prison, he was released in 1932. On 18 April 1940, McCoy took his own life with an overdose of sleeping pills.

✪ FIGHTING TALK (9) ✪

"I'm scared every time I go into the ring, but it's how you handle it. What you have to do is plant your feet, bite down on your mouthpiece and say, 'Let's go'."
Mike Tyson

✪ LEAST POPULATED MEDAL ✪

With a mere 53,500 inhabitants, Bermuda became the least populated country to win a medal at an Olympiad when Clarence Hill won the bronze medal in boxing's heavyweight division at the 1976 Montreal Games.

✪ THE GREAT WHITE HOPE ✪

During the 1980s Gerry Cooney was the so-called "Great White Hope" in boxing's heavyweight division. On 11 June 1982, Cooney was given a shot at Larry Holmes's WBC belt, and the purse of $10 million offered to the challenger made it the richest fight in history at that time. The last white heavyweight champion of the world had been Sweden's Ingemar Johansson some 23 years earlier (defeating Floyd Patterson), and in the lead-up to the fight a lot of unsavoury racial undertones emerged. Indeed, it was boxing promoter Don King who first called Cooney the "Great White Hope". The fighters met in the ring in Las Vegas, Nevada, in what was one of the biggest closed-circuit/pay-per-view bouts in boxing history, broadcast live to in excess of 150 countries. The champion showed no mercy to his less experienced challenger and battered him incessantly for 12 rounds before Cooney's trainer, Victor Vallie, threw the towel in during round 13 to stop his man taking any further punishment. Up to his fight with Holmes no one had lasted more than eight rounds against Cooney. On 27 June 1987, Cooney was given a second shot at a world title when he met Michael Spinks, the former world heavyweight champion and reigning world light-heavyweight champion, in Atlantic City. Cooney was by now well past his best, and Spinks knocked him out in five rounds. Cooney fought his last ever bout on 15 January 1990, again in Atlantic City, where former world heavyweight champion George Foreman knocked him out in round 2. Wisely, Cooney decided to retire with a professional record of 28 wins (24 KOs) and 3 losses. In his spare time Cooney is involved with the "Hands are not for hitting" programme, which aims to stop domestic violence.

✑ THE FAB FOUR: LEONARD V. HEARNS (1) ✑

Fight three of the series saw the WBA world welterweight champion, Thomas Hearns, face Sugar Ray Leonard, the WBA champion, in a unification bout at Caesar's Palace, Las Vegas, on 16 September 1981. This fight was billed as a "Battle of Champions", with "The Hitman" yet to taste defeat. Hearns fought superbly and fully utilized his six-inch reach advantage to lead the bout on all of the judges' scorecards after the first 12 rounds. Leonard's trainer, the legendary Angelo Dundee, could be heard saying: "You're blowing it, son, you're blowing it," as Leonard slumped in his stool at the end of round 12. Sugar Ray got Dundee's forthright message loud and clear and in round 13 laid into Hearns like a man possessed before sensationally stopping him in round 14.

✑ TABLES TURNED ON TIGER ✑

On 20 May 1965, Dick Tiger sent Rubin "Hurricane" Carter to the canvas four times en route to claiming a 10-round decision in New York. The following year, on 25 April 1966, Emile Griffith sent Tiger to the floor in round 9 of their fight in New York, the first time in Tiger's career he landed on the canvas. Griffith went on to win the 15-round bout to claim the world middleweight title.

✑ MEXICO'S SALDIVAR ✑

Shortly after Mexico's Vicente Saldivar stopped Howard Winstone in 12 rounds in Mexico City to retain his world featherweight title on 12 October 1967, he announced his retirement from the sport, aged only 24. Saldivar had first won the world title on 26 September 1964, when he upset the defending world featherweight champion Sugar Ramos with a 12th-round knockout. Three months after Saldivar abdicated his crown Winstone received recognition from the WBC as their featherweight champion. Meanwhile, Saldivar changed his mind about retirement, but lost his WBA world championship belt to Raul Rojas on 28 March 1968. Then, following another sabbatical from boxing, he returned to the ring on 18 July 1969 and won a 10-round unanimous decision over ex-champion Jose Legra. On 9 May 1970, he regained the world featherweight title following a 15-round unanimous decision over Johnny Famechon, only to lose the belt again seven months later when he was beaten by Kuniaki Shibata. He ended his professional career with a record of 37 wins (26 KOs) and 3 defeats.

✪ CHAMP FLEES PRISON SENTENCE ✪

On 13 May 1913, the reigning world heavyweight champion Jack Johnson found himself in court in Chicago charged with violating the Mann Act. It was alleged that Johnson took Belle Schreiber across State lines for immoral purposes. Although Johnson was found guilty only of inter-state travel with improper intent, on 4 June 1913 he was sentenced to a year in prison and a $1,000 fine. Johnson was still on bail when on 1 July 1913 he fled Chicago and set sail from Montreal aboard the *Carinthea* bound for France. The fugitive Johnson returned to the USA on 20 July 1920 and surrendered himself to federal agents. He was sent to the US Penitentiary, Leavenworth, to serve his sentence and on 9 July 1921 he was released. On 26 September 2008, the US Congress recommended that Johnson be given a presidential pardon. The Congressional resolution urged President George W. Bush to grant Johnson a pardon, claiming that the conviction was racially motivated after Johnson became the first black man to win the world heavyweight championship, with his 1908 win over Tommy Burns. The resolution went on to say that Johnson was frowned upon for having disposed of every "Great White Hope" who tried to take the belt from him, and because of his relationships with white women. In the words of Peter King, the House of Representatives member who penned the resolution, "He was a victim of the times and we need to set the record straight – clear his name – and recognize him for his groundbreaking contribution to the sport of boxing." The resolution was rejected by Bush, but a further appeal has been made to President Barack Obama.

✪ WHO KILLED DAVEY MOORE? ✪

Davey Moore was scheduled to fight Sugar Ramos in July 1962 at Dodger Stadium in Los Angeles, but the bout had to be postponed when a torrential rainstorm hit LA on the day of the fight. The bout was rearranged for 21 March 1963 and was shown live on television across the USA. In round 10 Ramos connected with a powerful right hook to Moore's head and he fell backwards to the floor, hitting the base of his neck on the bottom rope on the way. When he failed to make the count the referee awarded the fight to Ramos. Shortly after the contest ended Moore spoke to the television network, but when he got to his dressing-room he lapsed into a coma and was immediately taken to White Memorial Hospital, Los Angeles. Two days later he died of a brainstem injury. His death prompted much debate over the safety of the sport, Benny "Kid" Paret having died nine days after his fight with Emile Griffith almost exactly a year earlier.

◈ *RING MAGAZINE* FIGHTER OF THE YEAR ◈

The world's most famous magazine on boxing, *Ring Magazine*, was established in 1922. Six years after its formation (1928) the popular magazine introduced its "Fighter of the Year" award, which remains one of the most coveted awards in professional boxing. The award is a gold and silver medal and is presented to the boxer who during the previous year "earned the esteem of the sports public" through both his conduct and his fighting qualities. The following is a list of *Ring Magazine's* Fighters of the Year:

Year	Winner	Year	Winner
1928	Gene Tunney	1958	Ingemar Johansson
1929	Tommy Loughran	1959	Ingemar Johansson
1930	Max Schmeling	1960	Floyd Patterson
1931	Tommy Loughran	1961	Joe Brown
1932	Jack Sharkey	1962	Dick Tiger
1933	NO AWARD	1963	Cassius Clay
1934*	Tony Canzoneri	1964	Emile Griffith
	Barney Ross	1965	Dick Tiger
1935	Barney Ross	1966	NO AWARD
1936	Joe Louis	1967	Joe Frazier
1937	Henry Armstrong	1968	Nino Benvenuti
1938	Joe Louis	1969	Jose Napoles
1939	Joe Louis	1970	Joe Frazier
1940	Billy Conn	1971	Joe Frazier
1941	Joe Louis	1972*	Muhammad Ali
1942	Ray Robinson		Carlos Monzon
1943	Fred Apostoli	1973	George Foreman
1944	Beau Jack	1974	Muhammad Ali
1945	Willie Pep	1975	Muhammad Ali
1946	Tony Zale	1976	George Foreman
1947	Gus Lesnevich	1977	Carlos Zarate
1948	Ike Williams	1978	Muhammad Ali
1949	Ezzard Charles	1979	Sugar Ray Leonard
1950	Ezzard Charles	1980	Thomas Hearns
1951	Ray Robinson	1981*	Sugar Ray Leonard
1952	Rocky Marciano		Salvador Sanchez
1953	Bobo Olson	1982	Larry Holmes
1954	Rocky Marciano	1983	Marvin Hagler
1955	Rocky Marciano	1984	Thomas Hearns
1956	Floyd Patterson	1985*	Marvin Hagler
1957	Carmen Basilio		Donald Curry

Year	Winner	Year	Winner
1986	Mike Tyson	2001	Bernard Hopkins
1987	Evander Holyfield	2002	Vernon Forrest
1988	Mike Tyson	2003	James Toney
1989	Pernell Whitaker	2004	Glen Johnson
1990	Julio Cesar Chavez	2005	Ricky Hatton
1991	James Toney	2006	Manny Pacquiao
1992	Riddick Bowe	2007	Floyd Mayweather Jr.
1993	Michael Carbajal	2008	Manny Pacquiao
1994	Roy Jones Jr.	2009	Manny Pacquiao
1995	Oscar De La Hoya	2010	Floyd Mayweather Jr.
1996	Evander Holyfield	2011	Manny Pacquiao
1997	Evander Holyfield	2012	Manny Pacquiao
1998	Floyd Mayweather Jr.	2013	Floyd Mayweather Jr.
1999	Paulie Ayala	2014	Manny Pacquiao
2000	Felix Trinidad	* = *Award shared*	

❧ WHEN THE USA CAME SECOND ❧

Between 1885 and 1972 only five world heavyweight champions were not from North America (Tommy Burns was Canadian):

Boxer	Born in	Years champion
Bob Fitzsimmons	England	1896 & 1897–99
Georges Carpentier	France	1914
Max Schmeling	Germany	1930–32
Primo Carnera	Italy	1933–34
Ingemar Johansson	Sweden	1959-60

❧ RULE BRITANNIA ❧

James "Jem" Mace was born on 8 April 1831 in the English village of Beeston in Norfolk. As well as being the last great bare-knuckle fighter of the nineteenth century, his career of 35 years is the longest of any English professional boxer. On 10 May 1870, Mace fought fellow Englishman Tom Allen at St Charles's Theatre in LaSalle's Landing (later renamed Kenner), near New Orleans, Louisiana, in what was the first heavyweight championship prize fight held in the USA. The contest was billed as a "World Championship Fight featuring the Champion of England [Mace] versus the Champion of America [Allen]". Mace, who was 39 years old and concentrating more on his show business career than fighting, won the fight in round 10, when the 29-year-old, Birmingham-born Allen could no longer continue, having suffered a dislocated shoulder during a fall.

❦ THE WHITE BUFFALO IS STRIPPED ❧

Francois Botha, nicknamed the"White Buffalo", beat Axel Schulz in 12 rounds in Stuttgart, Germany, on 9 December 1995 to claim the vacant IBF world heavyweight title. Botha was then stripped of his belt after testing positive for the banned steroid Nandrolone. Despite claims that he had been prescribed the drug for an injury to his arm, the result of his fight against Schulz was declared a no contest and he had to hand back the IBF belt. Botha went on to fight other world champions, including Michael Moorer, Mike Tyson, Shannon Briggs, Lennox Lewis and Wladimir Klitschko, but lost to them all.

❦ A QUICK UNIFICATION BOUT ❧

Mike Tyson stopped Bruce Seldon in the opening round of their bout in Las Vegas, Nevada, on 7 September 1996 to regain the WBA world heavyweight title, unifying the WBA and WBC titles.

❦ THE BOXER WHO JUST LOVED TO BOX ❧

Battling Levinsky (born Barney Lebrowitz) was the world light-heavyweight champion from 24 October 1916 to 11 October 1920 and was the type of boxer who just simply loved to fight. In 1914 he fought an astonishing 37 bouts, nine in January alone and six in the one week, and on New Year's Day 1910 he fought three 10-round contests at three different venues across New York City. Battling would just about fight anyone, any time, any place and any weight. One evening he took his girlfriend to the opera in New York but when he arrived at the opera house he received a telephone call from his manager informing him that he had a fight for him that night. Battling did not have a scheduled fight that evening, but when a boxer withdrew from a card in New York, Levinsky's manager had no hesitation in putting his man forward as a late replacement. Battling jumped in a cab and made his way to the fight, grabbing someone else's gloves as he arrived at the arena. Having stopped his opponent in round 2, he had a quick shower, hailed a cab and went back to the opera house to join his girlfriend for the remaining part of the performance. It is often claimed that Levinsky had in excess of 500 bouts during his professional career, although his official statistics give him a professional record of 287 bouts – 192 wins (34 KOs), 52 losses, 34 draws and 9 no decisions. Levinsky, a proud Jew, was inducted into the International Boxing Hall of Fame and the International Jewish Sports Hall of Fame.

MASS BRAWL AT THE GARDEN

Following Riddick Bowe's victory by disqualification against Andrew Golota in seven rounds at Madison Square Garden, New York, on 11 July 1996, fighting broke out in the arena between the two camps, with both sets of fans joining in.

Did You Know That?
On 18 March 1991, Mike Tyson stopped Razor Ruddock in seven rounds in Las Vegas, Nevada and after the fight a mass brawl took place in the ring.

A DESERT CLASSIC

Paulie Ayala beat Johnny Tapia in 12 rounds in Las Vegas, Nevada to win the WBA world bantamweight title on 26 June 1999. The bout was named the Fight of the Year for 1999.

THE CHEATING BOXER AND TRAINER

Luis Resto caused a huge upset in the ring on 16 June 1983 when he defeated the highly rated and undefeated welterweight Billy Collins Jr. on the undercard of the Roberto Duran v. Davey Moore bout at Madison Square Garden, New York. When Collins's father walked over to congratulate Resto he shook his glove and to his amazement could feel Resto's hand. He immediately called the referee, and when Resto's gloves were examined they were found to have almost no padding, his trainer Panama Lewis having removed an inch of padding from them. During the bout Collins suffered a torn iris, leaving him with permanently blurred vision which meant the end of his boxing career. Resto and Lewis were handed lifetime bans from the sport. Sadly, on 6 March 1984, Collins Jr. died, aged 22, when he crashed his car while under the influence of alcohol. At a press conference in 2008, Resto not only admitted to knowing that his trainer had tampered with his gloves but that he had done so on at least two other occasions.

COOPER'S NEAR MISS

Despite sending Evander Holyfield to the canvas in round 3 of their bout in Atlanta, Georgia, on 23 November 1991, Bert Cooper was stopped in seven rounds by the reigning WBC world heavyweight champion, who retained his belt.

HAGLER AVENGES LOSS TO THE WORM

Marvin Hagler knocked out Willie "The Worm" Monroe in round 12 of their fight in Boston, Massachusetts, on 15 February 1977 to avenge a previous hometown 10-round loss to Monroe in Philadelphia the previous year.

WHEN THE TRUTH ENDED

On 16 January 1993, Tommy Morrison stopped Carl "The Truth" Williams in eight rounds in Reno, Nevada. Williams retired in 1997 with a professional record of 30 wins (21 KOs) and 10 losses. Williams is best known for his abortive crack at Mike Tyson's world heavyweight crown when the champion knocked him out in the opening round without Williams even throwing a punch.

BABY-FACED BOXER

James "Jimmy" Archibald McLarnin was born in Hillsborough, County Down, on 19 December 1907 but emigrated with his family to Canada in 1910. The young Irishman took up boxing at the age of 10 when he was forced by a rival boy to fight him for his lucrative newspaper-selling pitch in Vancouver. When he was 13 years old McLarnin impressed former professional boxer Charles "Pop" Foster so much that Foster built a makeshift gymnasium for McLarnin to train in, convinced that one day he would be a world champion. On 4 July 1925, McLarnin, now a bantamweight and nicknamed "Baby Face" and the "Belfast Sprinter", beat the legendary world flyweight champion Pancho Villa in 10 rounds in Oakland, Los Angeles. He got his first world title shot on 21 May 1928 but lost the world lightweight championship bout to defending champion Sammy Mandell in New York. It would be another five years before he got a second world title shot, despite having beaten Mandell twice in the intervening period. McLarnin took on and beat the reigning world welterweight champion Young Corbett III, knocking him out in round 1 in Los Angeles on 29 May 1933, but lost his belt in his first defence against Barney Ross exactly one year later on a 15-round split decision in Long Island. McLarnin regained his title in their next match four months later, and in their third match-up on 28 May 1935 Ross beat the champion with a narrow points decision. In November 1936, McLarnin retired with a record of 62 wins, 11 losses, 3 draws and 1 no decision. In 1996 *Ring Magazine* voted him the fifth-greatest welterweight of all time.

❦ FIGHTING TALK (10) ❧

"There's only one legend. That's me ..."
Roberto Duran

❦ DON'T MESS WITH ARCHIE ❧

Remarkably, the legendary Archie Moore's professional boxing record shows two knockout wins over professional wrestlers in what were actual professional wrestling events. In 1956 Moore beat "Professor" Roy Shire, and seven years later defeated "Iron" Mike DiBiase, the stepfather of the 1980s wrestling star Ted "Million Dollar Man" DiBiase. Both match-ups were staged, with Moore refereeing wrestling matches in which the loser (Shire and DiBiase) blamed Moore's officiating for costing them the match and ended up challenging Moore to a fight in the ring, which Moore naturally accepted. Moore stopped both men in round 3.

❦ BOX OFFICE ROCKY ❧

In the Rocky movies two real-life boxers made appearances, Joe Frazier in *Rocky* and Mike Tyson in *Rocky VI*, while the real-life sports presenter Brian Kenny (ESPN's *Sports Center*) had a part in *Rocky VI*. The fight entrance for *Rocky VI*, when Rocky comes out before his bout with Mason Dixon, was filmed during the world middleweight championship rematch between Jermain Taylor and Bernard Hopkins on 4 December 2005, with Taylor winning on points (115–113 on all three judges' cards) after 12 rounds.

❦ UPSET FIGHT OF THE YEAR ❧

On 4 September 1992, Britain's Kirkland Laing (nicknamed the "Gifted One") caused a major upset when he defeated Roberto Duran by a unanimous decision over 10 rounds in Detroit, Michigan. Going into the fight, "Hands of Stone" Duran had notched up an impressive record of 74 wins, with only three defeats (all three losses to future Boxing Hall of Fame opponents), and many in the crowded arena expected Duran to knock out his opponent in the early rounds. On the night, however, despite all of his street-fighting qualities Duran was no match for the hungry Laing. *Ring Magazine* chose the fight as its "Upset Fight of the Year". In his next fight Laing was knocked out by the relatively unknown Fred Hutchings, while Duran went on to win world titles at light-middleweight and middleweight.

13 Sep 50 Losing on points, world middleweight champion Jake LaMotta kept his title by knocking out Laurent Dauthuille with 13 seconds remaining in the bout in Detroit.

10 Jul 51 Randy Turpin caused a sensational upset when he beat the defending champ, Sugar Ray Robinson, over 15 rounds in London to become the new middleweight champion of the world. It was only Robinson's second loss in 133 fights.

31 Dec 52 In round 7 of their bout in Coral Gables, Florida, Danny Nardico floored Jake LaMotta, the first time in 103 fights that LaMotta had been sent to the canvas. Nardico surprisingly won the contest when LaMotta was unable to answer the bell for the eighth round.

15 May 53 Rocky Marciano retained his world heavyweight title by knocking out Jersey Joe Walcott in the opening round in Chicago.

2 Apr 54 Bobo Olson beat the reigning world welterweight champion, Kid Gavilan, in 15 rounds in Chicago to retain his world middleweight title.

9 Dec 55 Former world welterweight and middleweight champion Sugar Ray Robinson met the reigning world middleweight champ, Bobo Olson, as a 3–1 underdog in Chicago. Sugar Ray was 31 when he had retired as middleweight champion on 18 December 1952, but he knocked out Olsen in the second round to begin his third reign as world champion.

30 Sep 56 Ingemar Johansson knocked out Franco Cavicchi in the 13th round of their fight in Bologna, Italy, to win the European heavyweight title.

23 Sep 57 Reigning world welterweight champion Carmen Basilio beat Sugar Ray Robinson in 15 rounds in the Bronx, New York and claimed Sugar Ray's world middleweight belt.

15 Sep 58 George Chuvalo knocked out James J. Parker in the first round of their bout in Toronto, Canada, to win the Canadian heavyweight title.

12 Jan 59 Henry Cooper beat Brian London in 15 rounds in London to claim the British and Empire heavyweight titles.

☙ GOING THROUGH THE PAIN BARRIER ❧

On 14 July 1916, Jack Dempsey and John Lester Johnson fought out a 10-round, no-decision fight in New York despite the fact that Dempsey was suffering from two broken ribs.

❧ JACK JOHNSON ❧

Arthur John "Jack" Johnson, nicknamed "The Galveston Giant", was born on 31 March 1878 in Galveston, Texas. He started fighting when he was just 13 years old while already working as a docker. He developed a very distinctive boxing style, his method being to wait patiently for his opponent to make a mistake, which he immediately and relentlessly pounced upon. By 1902 he had fought more than 50 times, against white opponents as well as black. On 3 February 1903 Johnson entered the ring for his first title fight and defeated "Denver" Ed Martin over 20 rounds to win the "Negro-Heavyweight World Championship". However, his hopes of winning the world heavyweight championship were thwarted when the reigning champion, Gentleman James J. Jeffries, denied him a shot at the title. Indeed, it took 11 years for Johnson to get one, and only after chasing the champion, the Canadian Tommy Burns, halfway around the world. The bout took place at Rushcutter's Bay, Sydney, on 26 December 1908, and Johnson stopped Burns to become the first black world heavyweight champion.

This defeat of Burns was deeply unpopular with white America, and Johnson faced a campaign of hatred and vilification, while the search was on for the next white challenger. Stanley Ketchel, the world middleweight champion, came forward, in Colma, California, and floored Johnson in round 12, but the champion got up and knocked him out with his next punch. The public cried out for Jeffries to come out of retirement and fight Johnson, which he did in Reno, Nevada, on 4 July 1910. However, Jeffries was battered mercilessly by Johnson before being knocked out in round 15. Johnson's next title defence came exactly two years later when he met "Fireman" Jim Flynn in Las Vegas, where Flynn was disqualified in round 9. It was Johnson's last fight as the world champion on home soil.

White America wanted to see the end of Johnson and seized on any opportunity to bring him down. The champion was prosecuted under the Mann Act, which prohibited the transportation of women across US state lines for immoral purposes, and was sentenced to prison. Johnson fled to Europe before he could be incarcerated, and twice defended his title in Paris. Then, he later claimed, he agreed a deal with the boxing authorities to take a dive against Jess Willard in return for quashing his prison sentence. On 5 April 1915, Johnson fought Willard in Havana, Cuba, and was knocked out by his challenger in round 26.

Did You Know That?
He ended up in prison after the Willard fight, the authorities reneging on the deal.

⚔ TOMMY'S BELT ⚖

Tommy Morrison beat George Foreman in 12 rounds in Las Vegas on 7 June 1993 to win the vacant WBO world heavyweight title.

⚔ A SELECT BAND OF TWO ⚖

Apart from Joe Frazier, Muhammad Ali only ever fought one other boxer three times, Ken Norton. Ali fought Sonny Liston and Leon Spinks twice and George Foreman just once.

⚔ OUT COLD BUT HANGS ON FOR A DRAW ⚖

On 26 March 1909, Stanley Ketchel's 10-round fight against Philadelphia Jack O'Brien in New York was called a no contest by the judges – despite the fact that when the final bell was sounded O'Brien was out cold with his head resting in the resin box in his corner.

⚔ FOUR WEEKS, TWO TITLE DEFENCES ⚖

In the space of just over four weeks, from 13 March to 16 April 1952, Sugar Ray Robinson twice successfully defended his world middleweight title. First up was Carl "Bobo" Olson, whom the champion beat in 15 rounds in San Francisco, and then came Rocky Graziano, who was knocked out in the third round of their title bout in Chicago.

⚔ BOB'S REVENGE MISSION ⚖

On 24 August 1900, Bob Fitzsimmons hauled himself up from the canvas following a first-round knockdown by Tom "KO" Sharkey to beat his opponent in the second round of their fight in Coney Island, thereby avenging a disputed loss on a foul to Sharkey in 1896.

⚔ FIVE BOUTS IN ONE AFTERNOON ⚖

On 26 April 1975 in Toronto, Canada, the former world heavyweight champion George Foreman (who lost his belt to Muhammad Ali in his previous bout dubbed the "Rumble in the Jungle") took on five different opponents in one afternoon in three-round exhibition bouts. Foreman stepped into the ring with Charley Polite, Boone Kirkman, Terry Daniels, Jerry Judge and Alonzo Johnson. The hard-hitting Foreman knocked all five of his opponents out without breaking into a sweat.

NOT SUCH A HOT AMATEUR

Muhammad Ali lost to more amateur boxers (7) than professional boxers (5).

A VERY OLD SPORT

The earliest traces of boxing were discovered on the Greek island of Santorini. A fresco, showing two young boxers, is believed to date back as far as 1600 BC.

TUNNEY CALLS TIME

On 26 July 1929, Gene Tunney stopped Tom Heeney in the 11th round in the Bronx, New York, to retain his world heavyweight title, and soon after the fight ended Tunney retired as the undefeated world champion.

TIGER TOO SWEET FOR SUGAR RAY

On 19 January 1955, Ralph "Tiger" Jones caused a huge upset when he beat Sugar Ray Robinson in 10 rounds in Chicago. Jones, a loser in his five previous bouts, beat the former world welterweight and world middleweight champion in what was a comeback bout for Robinson, who had retired from boxing in December 1952.

ERNESTO QUITS IN EARNEST

Within a short period of time after defeating Alexis Arguello in 15 rounds in Panama City on 16 February 1974 to retain his WBA world featherweight title, Ernesto Marcel announced his retirement and vacated his belt.

REFEREE BETS ON KID

On 30 April 1904, the first major fight controversy of the twentieth century occurred in San Francisco, when the defending world welterweight champion, Joe Walcott, was disqualified by the referee Jim "Duck" Sullivan in round 20 of his bout against Dixie Kid. To the amazement of everyone in the crowd Sullivan declared Kid the winner on a foul, when it was apparent that Walcott was well in control of the fight. It was later discovered that Sullivan had bet on Kid to win.

⊗ FIGHTING TALK (11) ⊗

"Boxing is the ultimate challenge. There's nothing that can compare to testing yourself the way you do every time you step in the ring."
Sugar Ray Leonard

⊗ OLYMPIC FINAL TO WORLD TITLE FIGHT ⊗

In 1956 the USA's Pete Rademacher won the gold medal in the heavyweight boxing division at the Olympic Games in Melbourne, Australia. On 21 August 1957, in what was his professional debut, he went into the ring in Seattle against Floyd Patterson, who was putting his world heavyweight championship belt on the line. Going into the fight the challenger talked up his chances of stripping the champion of his belt, and in round 6 he sent shock waves around the arena when he sent Patterson to the canvas. However, the champion got to his feet, dusted himself down, and laid into Rademacher before knocking him out cold in the same round to retain his belt. In subsequent fights Rademacher lost to Zora Folley, Brian London and the former world lightweight champion, Archie Moore. However, he did beat George Chuvalo, Lamar Clark and, in his last fight, the former world middleweight champion, Carl "Bobo" Olson.

Did You Know That?
The Patterson v. Rademacher bout was the first and only time to date that a boxer challenged for a world heavyweight title when making his professional debut. It happened at light-flyweight in 1975.

⊗ EVEN SINATRA COULDN'T GET IN ⊗

The Muhammad Ali v. Joe Frazier world heavyweight championship bout at Madison Square Garden, New York, on 8 March 1971 was the hottest ticket in the Big Apple at the time, sold out months in advance of the two fighters going toe to toe in the ring. Not surprisingly, with neither fighter having previously tasted defeat, it became known as the "Fight of the Century". Indeed, a ticket for the bout was so hard to come by that the legendary singer and actor Frank Sinatra had to take photographs of the action for *Life Magazine* just to get a ringside seat. Don Dunphy, the legendary boxing commentator, and Hollywood actor Burt Lancaster delivered the live broadcast of the bout which saw Frazier hand Ali his first loss to retain his belt.

20TH-CENTURY TOP 10 LIGHTWEIGHTS

Rank	Boxer	Record (W–L–D)	KOs	Career
1.	Roberto Duran	102–15	70	1967–99
2.	Benny Leonard	85–5–1, 119 ND	69	1911–32
3.	Tony Canzoneri	137–24, 4 ND	44	1925–39
4.	Ike Williams	125–24–5	60	1940–56
5.	Joe Gans	120–8–9, 18 ND	85	1891–1909
=6.	Lou Ambers	86–8–6,	27	1932–41
=6.	Alexis Arguello	80–8	64	1968–96
8.	*Julio Cesar Chavez	107–6–2	86	1980–2005
9.	Beau Jack	83–24–5, 1 ND	40	1940–55
10.	Carlos Ortiz	61–7–1	30	1955–72

*= Active in 1999 (record to 1 June 2009)   Source: Associated Press, 30 December 1999

WORLD CHAMPION BY PUBLIC VOTE

On 15 November 1922, *The Boxing Blade* magazine ran a poll to determine who was deemed to be the first world junior-welterweight champion. Pinky Mitchell topped the voting. The new weight division (140lbs) fought hard to gain widespread acceptance in its early years, with the New York State Athletic Commission withdrawing its recognition of it in 1930. It was not until 12 March 1959 that it gained popularity, when Carlos Ortiz won the vacant title with a victory over Kenny Lane (who was unable to answer the bell for round 3).

RECORD NUMBER OF KNOCKDOWNS

On 26 December 1902, a boxing record was set which still exists today and will never be beaten. When Oscar Nelson fought Christy Williams at Hot Springs, South Dakota, the fighters knocked each other down a record 47 times. Nelson was floored five times, while Williams hit the canvas 42 times. He was finally knocked out in the 17th round.

A CLOSE SHAVE FOR PATTERSON

On 13 March 1961 – in their third meeting – Ingemar Johansson twice sent the reigning world heavyweight champion Floyd Patterson crashing to the canvas in the opening round at Miami Beach Convention Hall, Florida. But the champ got up both times and also managed to floor the challenger at the end of the round. Patterson knocked out Johansson in round 6 to retain his crown.

⚞ 20 GREATEST BOXING MOVIES ⚟

Title	Director	Year
Gentleman Jim	Raoul Walsh	1942
The Harder They Fall	Mark Robson	1956
Somebody Up There Likes Me	Robert Wise	1956
Kid Galahad	Phil Karlson	1962
Requiem for a Heavyweight	Ralph Nelson	1962
The Great White Hope	Martin Ritt	1970
Rocky	John G. Avildsen	1976
The Champ	Franco Zeffirelli	1979
Raging Bull	Martin Scorsese	1980
The Boxer	Jim Sheridan	1997
The Hurricane	Norman Jewison	1999
Rocky Marciano	Charles Winkler	1999
Ali	Michael Mann	2001
Carmen: The Champion	Lee Stanley	2001
Joe and Max	Steve James	2002
Against the Ropes	Charles S. Dutton	2004
Million Dollar Baby	Clint Eastwood	2004
Cinderella Man	Ron Howard	2005
Fighting Tommy Riley	Eddie O'Flaherty	2005
The Fighter	David O. Russell	2010

⚞ PUERTO RICO'S FIRST GREAT BOXER ⚟

In 1936, Sixto "El Gallito" Escobar became Puerto Rico's first ever boxing world champion when he knocked out Mexico's Baby Casanova to claim the world bantamweight title. Nearly 50 years later, Luis Ortiz was the first Puerto Rican to win a boxing medal at the Olympic Games when he claimed the silver medal at the 1984 Games in Los Angeles in the lightweight division, losing to the USA's Pernell Whitaker in the final.

Did You Know That?
Throughout his career Escobar was never knocked down or KO'd in a professional fight.

⚞ ROCKY STANDS ALONE ⚟

A famous sports writer once commented that if all the world heavyweight champions of all time were locked in a room, Marciano would be the one to walk out.

❧ MEXICAN SHOCKWAVE ☙

Mexico's 18-year-old Pipino Cuevas, born Jose Cuevas Gonzalez on 27 December 1957, caused a huge upset on 17 July 1976 when he knocked out the defending champion Angel Espada in the second round of their bout in Baja California, Mexico, to win the WBA world welterweight title. After successfully defending his title 11 times in four years, he was beaten by Thomas Hearns in the Hitman's home town, Detroit on 2 August 1980. Hearns knocked him out in round 2 of their bout, and after this defeat Pipino was never the same fighter again, losing to Roberto Duran in 1983 (stopped in the fourth round). Pipino retired in 1989 with a professional career record of 35 wins (31 KOs) and 15 defeats, having fought at a time when the welterweight division was a who's who of future boxing legends, including Wilfredo Benitez, Duran, Hearns, Sugar Ray Leonard and Carlos Palomino. In 2002 he was inducted into the International Boxing Hall of Fame.

❧ DOWN AND OUT ☙

Max Baer knocked out reigning world heavyweight champion Primo Carnera, in the 11th round of their fight in Long Island on 14 June 1934. Carnero was knocked down 11 times during the contest.

❧ THE THREE LOST ROUNDS OF BOXING ☙

Prior to their annual convention in 1982, the WBC announced that many rules concerning fighters' medical care before a bout needed to be changed to protect fighters' health. One of the most significant WBC rule changes was to reduce contests from 15 rounds to 12. Five years later both the WBA and IBF followed the WBC's lead, and when the WBO was formed in 1988 it too stipulated 12-round fights. In subsequent years the number of ropes in the ring were increased from five to six, and new medical procedures were also introduced to fighters' pre-fight checkups, including brain tests, lung tests and electrocardiograms. The WBC decided to act at their 1982 annual conference following the death of Duk-Koo Kim on 17 November 1982, four days after losing to Ray Mancini in Las Vegas.

❧ OUT BAZOOKA'D ☙

On 7 August 1983, Hector Camacho stopped Rafael "Bazooka" Limon in round 5 of their bout in San Juan, Puerto Rico, to claim the vacant WBC junior-lightweight title.

◎ THE FAB FOUR: HAGLER V. DURAN ◎

On 10 November 1983, Marvelous Marvin Hagler, the undisputed world middleweight champion, took on Roberto Duran, who was seeking his third world title belt at a different weight. Hagler was making the eighth defence of his title, none of the previous seven challengers having lasted more than 11 rounds. Very few gave Duran a chance of creating an upset, but Duran was fearless and could take a punch, which proved to be the case when both men battered each other mercilessly for the full 15 rounds. In the end the judges awarded the fight to Hagler by a unanimous decision, but by a narrow margin on each scorecard.

◎ THREE BELTS, THREE VACATIONS ◎

Alexis Arguello, nicknamed the "Explosive Thin Man", was the WBA world featherweight champion from 23 November 1974 to 1977, when he vacated his title (succeeded by Rafael Ortega); WBC world super-featherweight champion from 28 January 1978 to 1980, when he again vacated his title (succeeded by Rafael Limon); and the WBC world lightweight champion from 20 June 1981 to 1983, when for a third time he vacated his title (succeeded by Edwin Rosario).

◎ WHEN THE GREATEST FIRST APPEARED ◎

The crowd in the tiny arena in Louisville, Kentucky, who turned up to see a local kid fight on the night of 29 October 1960, had no idea that they were about to watch the professional debut of arguably the greatest ever exponent of boxing. Enter one Cassius Marcellus Clay, who announced himself as a star in the making by beating Tunney Morgan Hunsaker in six rounds. When the fight ended, Hunsaker did not even see the referee raise Clay's hand in the air, as both his eyes were swollen and shut, having absorbed so many blows during the bout. After the fight Hunsaker paid tribute to his opponent, saying: "Clay was as fast as lightning ... I tried every trick I knew to throw him off balance but he was just too good." In his autobiography, Muhammad Ali admitted that Hunsaker dealt him one of the hardest body blows he ever took in his entire professional career.

Did You Know That?
At the time of the fight Hunsaker was the chief of police of Fayetteville, West Virginia, having become, at 27, the youngest chief of police in the history of West Virginia.

⊙ THE HEAVYWEIGHT KNOCKOUT KING ⊗

On 4 January 1958, heavyweight boxer LaMar Clark made his professional debut and defeated John Hicks on points over six rounds in Cedar City, Utah. In his second professional bout just one week later he knocked out Willard Whitaker in round 2 in Cedar City. He proceeded to knock out his opponent in 40 of his next 41 bouts, and would have had a 100 per cent KO record but for Dick Tanner's retirement in round 2 of their bout on 10 November 1958 at the Fairgrounds Coliseum in Salt Lake City. Having notched up 43 consecutive wins from his first 43 outings, Clark finally lost to Bartolo Soni on 8 April 1960 by way of TKO in round 9 in Ogden, Utah. After experiencing the taste of defeat for the first time in his career he had three more fights, of which he won the first and lost the other two. His last ever fight, on 19 April 1961, was a second-round knockout defeat at the hands of a young Cassius Clay.

⊙ THE ROCK'S LAST STAND ⊗

On 21 September 1955, the reigning world heavyweight champion, Rocky Marciano, met the reigning world lightweight champion, Archie Moore, in the Bronx, New York, with Marciano placing his belt on the line. The move up in weight did not seem to be affecting Moore when he knocked Marciano to the canvas in round 2 – the second and last time Marciano was floored in his career. However, Marciano then sent Moore to the canvas five times before knocking him out in the ninth round to claim his 49th consecutive victory. It was his sixth successful title defence, and after the fight he announced his retirement. In his career Rocky had 49 fights and 49 wins, with 43 of them coming by way of knockout.

⊙ BAER KO'D ⊗

On 24 September 1935, Joe Louis knocked the former world heavyweight champion Max Baer to the canvas three times before knocking him out in round 4 of their bout in New York. The defeat was the first KO loss of Baer's career.

⊙ EVEN THE GREATEST FALL DOWN ⊗

On 10 February 1962, Cassius Clay was sent to the canvas for the first time in his career. However, he got back up on his feet and knocked out Sonny Banks in the fourth round of their fight in New York.

✺ JESUS IS BORN AGAIN ✺

In November 1981, Esteban De Jesus, the WBC world lightweight champion from 8 May 1976 to 21 January 1978, was convicted of murdering a 17-year-old over a traffic dispute. He was sentenced to life in jail in his native Puerto Rico. During his incarceration he took up baseball and was good enough to make the Puerto Rico penal system all-star team three times. In 1984 De Jesus became a born-again Christian and changed his life completely, becoming a preacher, and after it was discovered in prison that he had Aids, he was pardoned and released. However, it was apparent from his state of health that De Jesus did not have long to live, and so he returned home to spend his last days with his family. Roberto Duran, who fought De Jesus three times, losing once, visited De Jesus at his home in Puerto Rico and lifted his old adversary out of bed and hugged and kissed him, an event witnessed by another boxer, Jose Torres. Duran told his daughter to kiss De Jesus too, which she did, leaving Torres almost speechless at a time when so little was known yet, and so many fears existed about Aids. Esteban De Jesus died on 11 May 1989, just one month after he was released. He had a professional career record of 57 wins (32 KOs) and 5 losses.

✺ THE PERFECT PUNCH ✺

Gene Fullmer beat Sugar Ray Robinson in 15 rounds in New York on 2 January 1957 to win the world middleweight title. Four months later, 1 May 1957, Sugar Ray reclaimed it when he landed a left hook (referred to by commentators at the time as "the perfect punch") to the champion's jaw to knock out Fullmer in the fifth round of their title fight in Chicago and win the world middleweight title for a record fourth time.

✺ THE PUNCH THAT SHOOK NEW YORK ✺

When Joe Louis fought Paulino Uzcudun in New York on 14 December 1935, he hit him with a punch so hard in round 4 that it sent his opponent's teeth through his mouthpiece and upper lip. With blood gushing from Uzcudun's mouth, the referee stopped the contest. Louis described the punch as "the hardest punch I ever threw".

Did You Know That?
Up until he fought Louis, Uzcudun had never been knocked down or out before.

ᚖ FIGHTING TALK (12) ᚖ

"A champion shows who he is by what he does when he's tested. When a person gets up and says 'I can still do it', he's a champion."
Evander Holyfield

ᚖ MAKE YOUR MIND UP ᚖ

A young Cassius Clay sent a major tremor around the boxing fraternity when he stopped Sonny Liston in round 7 of their bout in Miami Beach, Florida on 25 February 1964 to win the world heavyweight title. Not long after the fight Clay went through two name changes, briefly to Cassius X and finally to Muhammad Ali.

ᚖ UNFAIR DECISION ᚖ

One of boxing's worst ever decisions was made in Seoul, South Korea, on 3 October 1967, when the judges awarded the home favourite, Ki-Soo Kim, a split-decision victory over 15 rounds against Freddie Little to retain his world light-middleweight title. Kim had turned professional in 1961 and won the world title when he defeated the defending champion, Nino Benvenuti, by a split decision in 1966.

ᚖ DISASTER IN LAS VEGAS ᚖ

On 13 November 1982, Ray "Boom-Boom" Mancini, the reigning WBA world lightweight champion, defended his title against South Korea's Duk-Koo Kim in an outdoor arena at Caesar's Palace, Las Vegas. Kim went into the world title bout with a 17–1–1 professional record, having won 12 fights on the bounce. The two fighters fought a bruising toe-to-toe contest, which ended when Mancini sent Kim crashing to the canvas inside 19 seconds of round 14. Kim banged his head hard on the floor, and although he somehow managed to rise unsteadily to his feet, the referee Richard Green stopped the fight and Mancini retained his title by TKO. Within minutes of the fight ending Kim lapsed into a coma and was taken to the hospital, where he underwent brain surgery. He died four days later. Kim's mother had flown from her home in South Korea to the USA to be at her son's bedside, and within three months she too was dead, having drunk a bottle of pesticide. On 1 July 1983, Richard Green took his own life. Meanwhile, Mancini was never the same fighter again and blamed himself for Kim's death. Later in July 1983, Kim's fiancée, Young Mee Lee, gave birth to their son, Chi Wan Kim.

20 Jun 60   When Floyd Patterson knocked out Ingemar Johansson with a thunderous left hook to the jaw in round 5 of their fight in New York, he became the first man to regain the world heavyweight championship belt.

4 Mar 61   Gene Fullmer met Sugar Ray Robinson for the fourth and final time and claimed a 15-round decision in Las Vegas to retain his world middleweight title. Fullmer's record against Sugar Ray was 2–1–1.

15 Nov 62   A 20-year-old Cassius Clay stopped the legendary Archie Moore (aged 48) in the fourth round of their light-heavyweight bout in Los Angeles.

18 Jun 63   Cassius Clay travelled to London to fight Britain's Henry Cooper. With his famous left hook Cooper sent Clay to the canvas in round 4 of their bout, but Clay got up to stop his opponent in the fifth round when Cooper was badly cut.

28 Feb 64   Rubin "Hurricane" Carter beat Jimmy Ellis in 10 rounds in New York.

10 Nov 65   A bumper crowd turned up to see what proved to be Sugar Ray Robinson's 201st and final bout of his professional career. Robinson, a pro for 26 years, lost a 10-round decision to Joey Archer in Pittsburgh and announced his retirement from the sport the following month.

1 Jun 66   Having beaten the undefeated Eder Jofre in 15 rounds in Nagoya, Japan, on 17 May 1965 to claim the world bantamweight title, Fighting Harada beat his main adversary once again, this time on a 15-round split decision in Tokyo to retain his belt. Harada's two wins over Jofre are the only defeats in Jofre's 78-fight career.

22 Oct 66   Carlos Ortiz stopped Sugar Ramos in round 5 of their bout in Mexico City to retain his world lightweight title.

19 Jul 67   Joe Frazier stopped George Chuvalo in the fourth round of their bout in New York, the first time Chuvalo did not go the distance in a fight.

3 Feb 68   Jerry Quarry stopped Thad Spencer in 12 rounds in Oakland, California, during their WBA heavyweight elimination tournament bout.

6 Dec 69   Sonny Liston sent Leotis Martin to the floor in round 4 of their bout for the vacant NABF heavyweight title in Las Vegas, and Liston was comfortably winning the contest on points when suddenly Martin knocked him out in the ninth round.

✺ BOXING'S FIRST $1M DOLLAR GATE ✺

Boxing's first ever $1 million dollar gate took place on 2 July 1921 in Jersey City. Needless to say the fight was for the world heavyweight championship, with Jack Dempsey putting his belt up for grabs against the pride of French boxing, Georges Carpentier. The champion knocked out his challenger in the fourth round in front of 80,183 fans who paid a total of $1,789,238 to see the bout.

Did You Know That?
The Dempsey v. Carpentier fight was the first world championship title fight to be broadcast live on radio.

✺ DON'T TAKE NO JIBBER-JABBER ✺

After becoming world heavyweight champion in February 1978, Leon Spinks hired a young "Mr T" as his personal bodyguard.

✺ WHEN THE CAVEMAN ROARED ✺

William "Caveman" Lee got off the floor to knock out John LoCicero in round 5 of their titanic battle in Detroit, Michigan, on 9 July 1981 in what was later named the Fight of the Year.

✺ WHEN JESUS BECAME WORLD CHAMPION ✺

On 18 April 1970, Ruben Olivares outpointed Jesus Castillo Aguillera (better known as Chucho Castillo) to retain his WBA and WBC world bantamweight title. The fight was the beginning of a fierce rivalry between the two Mexican boxers which saw them fight three times over a total of 44 rounds. On 16 October 1970, Castillo inflicted the first loss of Olivares's career to claim both belts in Inglewood, Los Angeles. The referee stopped the bout in round 14 with the defending champion suffering from a bad cut over his eye. Following a non-title win, Castillo and Olivares met for a third time on 3 April 1971, which saw Olivares reclaim the WBA and WBC titles by outpointing Castillo despite suffering an early knockdown. Castillo continued to fight on after losing his titles, but his record following his trilogy of bouts with Olivares was less than impressive: 5 wins and 7 losses. He announced his retirement from the sport on 12 December 1975 with a career record of 46 wins (22 KOs), 18 losses and 2 draws. During his career he also won the bantamweight championship of Mexico.

✸ WHAT'S IN A NAME? ✸

The following is a list of some very famous boxers and the names they were born with:

Born		*Fought as*
Walker Smith	=	Ray Robinson
Henry Jackson	=	Henry Armstrong
Anthony Zeski	=	Tony Zale
Rocco Barbella	=	Rocky Graziano
Stanislaus Keicel	=	Stanley Ketchel
Richard Ihetu	=	Dick Tiger
Arnold Cream	=	Jersey Joe Walcott
Joseph Barrow	=	Joe Louis
Rocco Marchegiano	=	Rocky Marciano
Barnett Rosofsky	=	Barney Ross
Gerardo Gonzalez	=	Kid Gavilan
Benjamin Leiner	=	Benny Leonard
Judah Bergman	=	Jackie (Kid) Berg
William Guiglermo Papaleo	=	Willie Pep
Eligio Sardinias Montalbo	=	Kid Chocolate
Cassius Marcellus Clay, Jr	=	Muhammad Ali
Dwight Braxton	=	Dwight Muhammad Qawi
Maxwell Antonio Loach	=	Matthew Saad Muhammad
Edward Lee Gregory	=	Eddie Mustafa Muhammad
Oscar Mattheus Nielsen	=	Battling Nelson
Jose Isidro Cuevas Gonzalez	=	Pipino Cuevas

✸ ONLY A KO IS OK ✸

In some jurisdictions in the early years of the last century, boxing titles could only change hands if the champion was knocked out by his challenger, while a non-KO championship fight was often classed as a "no decision". In other areas, local newspapers declared the winner.

✸ BATTLING OUT-BATTLED ✸

On 11 October 1920, France's Georges Carpentier knocked out the defending world light-heavyweight champion Battling Levinsky in the fourth round of their title clash to claim the belt in Jersey City. Battling had won the world light-heavyweight championship on 24 October 1916, defeating the reigning champion Jack Dillon. His loss to Carpentier was his first defeat in 59 bouts in almost four years.

⚞ JOE LOUIS ⚟

Joseph Louis Barrow, nicknamed the "Brown Bomber", was born on 13 May 1914 in Lafayette, Alabama. When he was 12 years old his stepfather moved the family north to Detroit. Joe's mum gave him the money for violin lessons, but Louis spent the money on boxing lessons instead. In 1933 he reached the finals of the American Championships, won the light-heavyweight title the following year and then decided to turn professional. With John Roxborough as his manager and Jack Blackburn as his trainer, Louis destroyed just about everyone who was put in front of him over the next three years, with the exception of Germany's Max Schmeling, who ended Louis' unbeaten run with a 12th-round knockout in June 1934. On 22 June 1937 Louis was given his first shot at the heavyweight world title when James J. Braddock agreed to face him in Chicago. Despite being sent to the canvas in the opening round, Louis got to his feet and stopped Braddock in round 8. Over the next 11 years Louis was unstoppable as he beat all challengers for his crown as he notched up 25 consecutive title defences. The list of unsuccessful challengers included Tommy Farr, Schmeling, Buddy Baer, Billy Conn and Jersey Joe Walcott (twice). In his fight with Schmeling in New York on 22 June 1938, Louis set out to exact revenge on the only man up to that point who had ever beaten him. Schmeling was the pride of Nazi Germany but Louis battered him into submission in only 124 seconds of their contest. To the dismay of the Nazi party, Schmeling's cries of pain could clearly be heard over the wireless as the champion mercilessly laid into his challenger.

Louis retired in 1949 as the undefeated world heavyweight champion but was forced back into the ring as a result of tax problems. In his comeback fight he lost to the NBA Champion Ezzard Charles in New York on 27 September 1950, and when Rocky Marciano knocked him out in 1951 he retired for good. The financial problems continued after his second retirement, but President Kennedy wrote off Louis' tax bills as a gesture of thanks from the country he had served so well in the Second World War. He was employed at Caesar's Palace, in Las Vegas, to greet their guests, but died in Las Vegas following a long bout of illness on 12 April 1981. Joe Louis had a proud record of 69 wins and just three defeats in his 72-fight professional career.

Did You Know That?
Braddock was paid a massive $300,000 for agreeing to fight Louis and was guaranteed a percentage of Louis' earnings for the next 10 years.

☜ FIGHTING TALK (13) ☞

"If they cut my bald head open, they will find one big boxing glove. That's all I am. I live it."
Marvelous Marvin Hagler

☜ SUGAR RAY LEONARD – FIGHT RECORD ☞

Record: 36 wins (25 by KO), 3 defeats, 1 draw

Date	*Opponent, City*	*Result*
5 Feb 1977	Luis Vega, Baltimore MD	W pts 6
14 May 1977	Willie Rodrigues, Baltimore MD	W pts 6
10 Jun 1977	Vinnie DeBarros, Hartford, CT	W TKO 3
24 Sep 1977	Frank Santore, Baltimore, MD	W KO 5
5 Nov 1977	Augustin Estrada, Las Vegas, NV	W KO 5
17 Dec 1977	Hector Diaz, Washington DC	W KO 2
4 Feb 1978	Rocky Ramon, Baltimore, MD	W pts 8
1 Mar 1978	Art McKnight, Dayton, OH	W TKO 7
19 Mar 1978	Javier Muniz, New Haven, CT	W KO 1
13 Apr 1978	Bobby Hayman, Landover, MD	W rtd 3
13 May 1978	Randy Milton, Utica, NY	W TKO 8
3 June 1978	Rafael Rodridguez, Baltimore, MD	W pts 10
18 July 1978	Dick Ecklund, Boston, MD	W pts 10
9 Sep 1978	Floyd Mayweather (Sr), Providence, RI	W TKO 10
6 Oct 1978	Randy Shields, Baltimore, MD	W pts 10
3 Nov 1978	Bernardo Prada, Portland, ME	W pts 10
9 Dec 1978	Armando Muniz, Springfield, MA	W rtd 6
11 Jan 1979	Johnny Gant, Landover, MD	W TKO 8
11 Feb 1979	Fernand Marcotte, Miami Beach, FL	W TKO 8
24 Mar 1979	Daniel Aldo Gonzalez, Tucson, AZ	W KO 1
21 Apr 1979	Adolfo Viruet, Las Vegas, NV	W pts 10
20 May 1979	Marcos Geraldo, Baton Rouge, LA	W pts 10
24 Jun 1979	Tony Chiaverini, Las Vegas, NV	W RTD 4
12 Aug 1979	Pete Ranzany, Las Vegas, NV	W TKO 4
28 Sep 1979	Andy Price, Las Vegas, NV	W KO 1
30 Nov 1979	*Wilfred Benitez, Las Vegas, NV	W TKO 15
31 Mar 1980	*Dave Green, Landover, MD	W KO 4
20 Jun 1980	*Roberto Duran, Montreal, Canada	W pts 15
25 Nov 1980	*Roberto Duran, New Orleans, LA	W TKO 8
28 Mar 1981	*Larry Bonds, Syracuse, NY	W TKO 10
25 Jun 1981	*Ayub Kalule, Houston, TX	W TKO 9
16 Sep 1981	*Thomas Hearns, Las Vegas, NV	W TKO 14

Date	Opponent, City	Result
15 Feb 1982	*Bruce Finch, Reno, NV	W TKO 3
11 May 1984	Kevin Howard, Worcester, MA	W TKO 9
6 Jun 1987	*Marvin Hagler, Las Vegas, NV	W pts 12
7 Nov 1988	*Donny Lalonde, Las Vegas, NV	W TKO 9
12 Jun 1989	*Thomas Hearns, Las Vegas, NV	D 12
7 Dec 1989	*Roberto Duran, Las Vegas, NV	W pts 12
9 Feb 1991	*Terry Norris, New York City, NY	W pts 12
1 Mar 1997	*Hector Camacho, Atlantic City, NJ	L TKO 5

* = World title fight

RIDDICK BOWE SAYS "NO DEAL"

On 13 November 1992, Riddick Bowe (nicknamed "Big Daddy" and "Sugar Man") met Evander "the Real Deal" Holyfield at the Thomas & Mack Center, Las Vegas, for Holyfield's IBF, WBA and WBC world heavyweight belts. Bowe became the undisputed world champion, taking a unanimous 12-rounds decision. The unification didn't last long because Bowe threw the WBC belt in a rubbish bin because he refused to meet their top contender Lennox Lewis.

ALI, THE CONSCIENTIOUS OBJECTOR

On 22 March 1967, Muhammad Ali knocked out Zora Folley in round 7 of their bout in New York to retain his WBA and WBC world heavyweight titles. However, a month later Ali was stripped of his NABF, WBA and WBC heavyweight titles for refusing to enlist in the US armed forces. Ali considered himself a conscientious objector and publicly stated: "War is against the teachings of the Holy Qur'an. I'm not trying to dodge the draft. We are not supposed to take part in no wars unless declared by Allah or The Messenger. We don't take part in Christian wars or wars of any unbelievers." Two months after his refusal to enlist Ali went on trial and was found guilty by the jury after just 21 minutes of deliberation. The judge sentenced Ali to five years in prison. However, it was not just in the ring that Ali was a fighter. He appealed to the Court of Appeals, which upheld the conviction. Eventually his case went before the US Supreme Court, which overturned the conviction in 1971.

Did You Know That?
Ali is also famously reported to have said the following in 1966: "I ain't got no quarrel with them Viet Cong. They never called me Nigger."

⚔ A UNIQUE ACHIEVEMENT ⚔

On 4 March 1901, reigning world middleweight champion Tommy Ryan made a successful defence of his crown by knocking out Tommy West in the 17th round of their contest at the Southern Athletic Club, Louisville, Kentucky. In 1892 Ryan had stopped West in the 14th round of a world welterweight title fight to retain his championship. With that 1901 defeat of West, Ryan holds the unique distinction of being the only fighter in boxing history to defend two different world titles against the same challenger in different centuries.

⚔ PUERTO RICO'S SECOND GREAT CHAMP ⚔

On 21 April 1962, Carlos Ortiz defeated Joe Brown over 15 rounds of boxing in Las Vegas, Nevada, to win the world lightweight title. Ortiz, from Puerto Rico, began his professional career in 1955 with a first-round knockout of Harry Bell in New York. On 12 June 1959, Ortiz faced Kenny Lane in New York for the vacant world junior-welterweight title, vacated by Tippy Larkin. Only a few months before this fight, Lane had dealt Ortiz the second loss of his career, winning a 10-round decision in Florida. However, on this occasion Ortiz knocked out Lane in round 2 to become the new junior-welterweight champion of the world. His victory meant that he became Puerto Rico's first world boxing champion since Sixto Escobar more than 30 years earlier, and only the second ever. On 1 September 1960 he lost his world junior-welterweight belt to Duilio Loi in Milan, Italy. Five years later, 10 April 1965, he lost his world lightweight title to Ismael Laguna in Rome, Italy before reclaiming it on 13 November 1965 in a rematch with Laguna. On 28 November 1966, Ortiz floored Flash Elorde for the first time in his career, knocking his opponent out in the 14th round of their bout in New York to retain his world lightweight title. Ortiz defended his world lightweight belt against the Dominican Republic's Carlos Cruz on 29 June 1968 but lost a 15-round decision in Cruz's home country. Cruz agreed to a rematch in San Juan, but on his way there he died in a plane crash. Ortiz continued boxing until Scotland's Ken Buchanan stopped him in six rounds at Madison Square Garden, when he retired. He ended his career with a record of 61 wins (30 KOs), 7 losses and 1 draw, with one bout declared a no contest.

Did You Know That?
Ortiz's loss to Buchanan was the only time he was stopped in his career.

20TH-CENTURY TOP 10 FEATHERWEIGHTS

Rank	Boxer	Record (W–L–D)	KOs	Career
1.	Willie Pep	230–11–1	65	1940–66
2.	Sandy Saddler	144–16–2	103	1944–56
3.	Salvador Sanchez	44–1–1	32	1975–82
4.	Tony Canzoneri	137–24–10, 4 ND	44	1925–39
5.	Chalky Wright	150–40–15	75	1928–48
=6.	Henry Armstrong	151–21–9	101	1931–45
=6.	Vicente Saldivar	38–3	27	1961–73
=8.	Wilfredo Gomez	44–3–1	42	1974–89
=8.	Azumah Nelson	39–5–2	29	1979–98
10.	Abe Attell	91–9–18, 46 ND	53	1900–17

Source: Associated Press, 30 December 1999

THE NAKED BOXER

In Newark, New Jersey, in 1942, Timmy Larkin was so focused on his bout with Tommy Cross that he forgot to put on his trunks before leaving the dressing-room. When his trainer disrobed him, Larkin stood in the middle of the ring wearing nothing but his boots, socks and gloves – much to the dismay of the ladies in the crowd.

THE GOD WHO INVENTED BOXING

In Ancient Greek culture, the god Apollo was regarded as the creator and guardian of the sport of boxing. According to some historians the purpose of the early bouts was not to knock out your opponent, but to remain unhurt until your opponent was exhausted and had to retire – which he signalled by raising two fingers in the air. It is said that on one occasion a Greek fighter avoided being hit for two days before his opponent packed it in.

SMOKIN' JOE'S GOLD

Joe Frazier won the heavyweight boxing gold medal at the 1964 Olympic Games in Tokyo. In 1967 Muhammad Ali (light-heavyweight gold medallist in 1960) was stripped of his world heavyweight championship belt after refusing to enlist in the US Army. The following year Frazier fought Buster Mathis for the vacant title and won it with an 11th-round knockout. During his career Frazier fought Ali three times, winning their first encounter in 1971 but losing the following two in 1974 and 1975.

❧ *THE RING* KNOCKOUT OF THE YEAR ❧

Year	Weight	Winner	Round	Loser
1989	Middleweight	Michael Nunn	1	Sumbu Kalambay
1990	Middleweight	Terry Norris	1	John Mugabi
1992*	Super-bantam	Kennedy McKinney	11	Welcome Ncita
1992*	Light-welter	Morris East	11	Akinobu Hiranaka
1993	Middleweight	Gerald McClellan	5	Julian Jackson
1994	Heavyweight	George Foreman	10	Michael Moorer
1995	Light-middle	Julio Cesar Vasquez	11	Carl Daniels
1996	Featherweight	Wilfredo Vasquez	11	Eloy Rojas
1997	Super-feather	Arturo Gatti	5	Gabriel Ruelas
1998	Light-heavy	Roy Jones Jr.	4	Virgil Hill
1999	Heavyweight	Derrick Jefferson	6	Maurice Harris
2000	Light-welter	Ben Tackie	10	Roberto Garcia
2001	Heavyweight	Lennox Lewis	4	Hasim Rahman
2002	Heavyweight	Lennox Lewis	8	Mike Tyson
2003	Featherweight	Rocky Juarez	10	Antonio Diaz
2004	Light-heavy	Antonio Tarver	2	Roy Jones Jr.
2005	Super-middle	Allan Green	1	Jaidon Codrington
2006	Heavyweight	Calvin Brock	6	Zuri Lawrence
2007	Flyweight	Nonito Donaire	5	Vic Darchinyan
2008	Light-welter	Kendall Holt	1	Ricardo Torres
2009	Junior-welter	Manny Pacquiao	2	Ricky Hatton
2010	Middleweight	Sergio Gabriel Martinez	2	Paul Williams
2011†	Bantamweight	Nonito Donaire	2	Fernando Montiel
2012	Welterweight	Juan Manuel Marquez	6	Manny Pacquiao
2013	Welterweight	Adonis Stevenson	1	Chad Dawson
2014	Light-middle	Andy Lee	5	John Jackson

* = *There was no award in 1991, but two in 1992.*

† = *Nonito Donaire's victory (2011) was a technical knockout*

❧ LUCKY TRUNKS ❧

On 8 June 1933, Max Schmeling, the former world heavyweight champion, stepped into the ring at Yankee Stadium, New York, as the 7–5 favourite to beat future champion Max Baer. Schmeling was Adolf Hitler's favourite sportsman, and when Baer entered the ring he sported a Star of David on his trunks, his father being half-Jewish. Baer stopped the German in round 10 with a technical knockout, and after his win said he would wear the "lucky" trunks in all of his fights.

❧ THE SAGINAW KID ☙

Kid Lavigne was born George Henry Lavigne on 6 December 1869 in Michigan. Nicknamed the "Saginaw Kid", he was the world lightweight champion from 1 June 1896 (defeating Dick Burge by a TKO) to 3 July 1899, when he lost his belt to Frank Erne. Lavigne turned professional in 1886 and in his first 48 fights he was undefeated (40 wins, 6 draws and 2 no contests). In 1894 he fought Andy Bowen and knocked him out. The following day, when Bowen was found dead, Lavigne was arrested by the police and initially charged with murder. However, it was decided that Bowen had hit his head on the wooden floor of the ring and subsequently died from his injuries, and Lavigne was cleared of any wrongdoing and released. In total he successfully defended his title six times, including a win over Joe Walcott in 1897, and ended his professional career with a record of 36 wins (20 KOs), 8 losses, 9 draws and 2 no contests. Lavigne died in 1928, and 70 years later he was inducted into the International Boxing Hall of Fame.

Did You Know That?
Lavigne's bout with Burge was the first to be fought under the Marquess of Queensberry Rules.

❧ WIFE TURNED TRAINER ☙

According to folklore, Rose Fitzsimmons, the wife of Bob Fitzsimmons, was partly responsible for her husband defeating James J. Corbett on 17 March 1897 in Carson City, Nevada, to win the world heavyweight title. The defending champion was a stone heavier than Fitzsimmons and battered his challenger for 13 rounds. The story goes that during round 14 Rose started to scream at her husband: "Hit the ribs, Bob! Hit the ribs!" Upon hearing his wife's instructions, Bob landed his famous solar plexus punch on the champion and stopped him in the 14th round.

❧ BAN ON ALI LIFTED ☙

In October 1970, Muhammad Ali's ban from boxing was lifted and he immediately arranged to fight the No. 1 contender for the world heavyweight title at the time, Jerry Quarry. Ali won the fight with a TKO in the third round, the referee stopping the fight when a cut over Quarry's eye made it almost impossible for him to see Ali. Quarry had to have 13 stitches in the cut.

⊗ FIGHTING TALK (14) ⊗

"To me, boxing is like a ballet – except there's no music, no choreography, and the dancers hit each other."
Jack Handy

⊗ NO RESPECT FOR THE CHAMPION ⊗

Lew Jenkins rocked the boxing world on 10 May 1940 when he stopped the reigning lightweight champion of the world, Lou Ambers, in the fourth round of their title fight in New York. Going into the fight the champion had rarely been floored in a fight before and had never been stopped, but his challenger showed no respect for this in taking his title. After Jenkins won the title he next fought the reigning world welterweight champion, Henry Armstrong, in a non-title contest two months later in New York. Armstrong stopped Jenkins in round 6.

⊗ CHAMPION STUNNED BY UNDERDOG ⊗

On 4 October 1940, the bookmakers made challenger Fritzie Zivic a long-shot outsider to defeat the reigning world welterweight champion and one of the best pound-for-pound fighters of his era, Henry Armstrong. The champion put his belt on the line and was as stunned as the crowd when Zivic beat him in 15 rounds to become the new world champion. Zivic fought Armstrong again for the title in New York on 17 January 1941, this time stopping the former champion in the 12th round.

⊗ WHEN GOLIATH BEAT DAVID ⊗

When the reigning world heavyweight champion, Primo Carnera, entered the ring in Miami on 1 March 1934 to defend his title against the former world light-heavyweight champion, Tommy Loughran, the champ weighed a massive 270lbs. Loughran weighed in at 184lbs but was no match for the Italian. Carnera's 86lbs weight advantage remains a world record for a heavyweight championship bout.

⊗ BOXING'S GREATEST FAN ⊗

John McNeill, who served as the Deputy Boxing Commissioner of New York from 1924 to 1936, estimated that he witnessed some 30,000 fights and 75,000 rounds of boxing.

❧ THE FAB FOUR: HEARNS V. DURAN ☙

The fifth contest of this remarkable series saw Roberto Duran and Thomas Hearns fighting for the WBC world super-welterweight championship in Las Vegas on 15 June 1984. Hearns, the defending champion, laid into Duran from the opening bell and his challenger did not know what hit him. Indeed, Duran was sent to the floor twice in the first round, at the end of which a dazed and confused challenger staggered to the wrong corner. Hearns, sensing victory, piled the pressure on Duran in round 2, bombarding Duran's head and body with crushing blows and knocking him out cold in one of the most sensational KOs in the history of professional boxing, to leave Duran lying face down on the canvas. It was a masterful performance of aggression and power from "The Hitman", who lived up to his name and retained his title in style.

❧ THE MARATHON BOXER ☙

According to the *Guinness Book of Records*, Bob Fitzsimmons's career as a professional boxer was the longest of all time, lasting from 1883 to 1914.

❧ THE MARATHON FIGHT ☙

On 7 September 1907, boxing history was made in Crawford, Nebraska, when middleweights Montana Jack Sullivan and Nat Dewey fought out a draw over 45 rounds of boxing. It was the only 45-round bout in boxing history to go the distance.

❧ THE LONGEST BOUT ☙

The longest ever bout between fighters with gloves and fought over three-minute rounds took place at the Olympic Club, New Orleans, on 6 April 1893. Andy Bowen and Jack Burke did battle for a mammoth 110 rounds, and when neither man had the strength to get off his stool for round 111, the referee declared the bout a draw. They split the $2,500 purse.

❧ THE LAST EVER 20-ROUND FIGHT ☙

The last ever scheduled 20-round bout in boxing history took place on 1 June 1971 in Oklahoma City. Brian Kelly stopped Alonzo Harris in 10 rounds.

✵ A CENTURY OF FIGHTS – 1970–79 ✵

29 Jun 70   Boxing fans turned out in numbers to see Sonny Liston's last ever fight. Liston stopped Chuck Wepner in 10 rounds in Jersey City.

8 Mar 71   In what turned out to be the fight of the decade, Joe Frazier faced Muhammad Ali at Madison Square Garden. Ali pounded away at the reigning world heavyweight champion in the early rounds, scoring well with the judges after bloodying and swelling Frazier's face. But Frazier fought back, sent Ali to the canvas in the 15th round and claimed a unanimous points decision to retain his crown.

17 Nov 72   Esteban De Jesus caused a huge upset when he floored Roberto Duran in the opening round of their non-title bout in New York en route to winning a 10-round decision. It was Duran's first defeat.

2 Jan 73   George Foreman sent Joe Frazier to the floor six times in the opening two rounds of their bout in Kingston, Jamaica, leading the referee to stop the fight and crown Foreman the new world heavyweight champion.

30 Oct 74   Muhammad Ali and George Foreman met for the "Rumble in the Jungle" in Kinshasa, Zaire. Once again Ali shocked the world when he took to the ropes and allowed Foreman to pound away at him, but the effort eventually wore Foreman down. In round 8 Ali knocked out the exhausted defending champion to win the world heavyweight title for a second time.

30 Jun 75   Carlos Monzon made his first and only appearance in the ring in the USA and stopped Tony Licala in 10 rounds in New York to retain his world middleweight title.

22 May 76   Victor Galindez put his WBA world lightweight belt on the line in Johannesburg, South Africa, against Richie Kates. The challenger had the champion in trouble, cut over both eyes and trailing on points, but with just one second remaining in round 15, the champion knocked out Kates to retain his title.

5 Nov 77   Ken Norton beat Jimmy Young in 15 rounds in an eliminator for the WBC world heavyweight title.

21 Jan 78   Roberto Duran re-unified the world lightweight division by knocking out Esteban De Jesus in round 12 of their bout in Las Vegas.

14 Jan 79   Wilfred Benitez beat Carlos Palomino in 15 rounds in San Juan to win the world welterweight title.

❧ BOXER MURDERS HIS WIFE ❧

On 26 November 1936, Billy Papke (nicknamed the "Illinois Thunderbolt"), the former world middleweight champion, shot and killed his estranged wife and then turned the gun on himself in Newport, California. He was 52 years old when he died.

Did You Know That?
When Papke lost his world middleweight belt to Stanley Ketchel he received such a battering in the bout that his wife did not recognize him when it was over.

❧ MANNY HONOURED ❧

In February 2008, reigning WBC super-featherweight champion Manny Pacquiao became the first athlete to be honoured with a commemorative postage stamp by the Philippine Postal Service.

❧ STOPPED BY A NUNN ❧

On 28 July 1988, Michael Nunn stopped Frank Tate in round 9 of their bout in Las Vegas to win the IBF world middleweight title.

❧ THE SPINKS JINX ❧

Michael Spinks, the former world light-heavyweight and world heavyweight champion, was nicknamed "Jinx" during his career, while his thunderous right hand punch became known as the "Spinks Jinx".

❧ THE BIG MAC WORLD CHAMPION ❧

Some years after former WBA and WBC world heavyweight champion Leon Spinks had retired from boxing he found himself working at the local YMCA in Columbus, Nebraska, and at McDonalds.

❧ WEAVING HIS MAGIC FIST ❧

Going into the 15th and final round of their WBA world heavyweight title bout in Knoxville, Tennessee, on 31 March 1980, Mike Weaver was trailing John Tate on points by a distance. However, in round 15 Weaver sent Tate crashing to the canvas to become champion.

⊗ JOE'S NEW YORK BOW ⊘

Joe Louis made his New York boxing debut on 25 June 1935 and annihilated the former world heavyweight champion, Primo Carnera, stopping the Italian in round 6.

⊗ SEVEN UP FOR LOUIS ⊘

When the legendary Joe Louis knocked out Lou Nova in the sixth round of their bout in New York on 29 September 1941, it was not only his 19th successful defence of his world heavyweight belt in a row; it was also his seventh successful defence for the year, which remains a heavyweight record today.

⊗ FAMOUS BOXING NICKNAMES (2) ⊘

Nickname	*Boxer*
The Brockton Blockbuster	Rocky Marciano
The Brown Bomber	Joe Louis
The Cincinnati Flash	Ezzard Charles
The Cinderella Man	James Braddock
The Clones Cyclone	Barry McGuigan
The Dark Destroyer	Nigel Benn
The Ding-a-Ling Man	Darnell Wilson
Dynamite	Michael Dokes
The Easton Assassin	Larry Holmes
El Terrible	Erik Morales
The Executioner	Bernard Hopkins
Explosive Thin Man	Alexis Arguello
Fireman	Jim Flynn
Gentleman	Jim Corbett
The Ghetto Wizard	Benny Leonard
Give 'em Hell	O'Neil Bell
The Golden Boy	Oscar de la Hoya
The Greatest	Muhammad Ali
Gunboat	Ed Smith
Hands of Stone	Roberto Duran
The Hispanic Causing Panic	Juan Lazcano
The Hitman	Tommy Hearns
The Hitman	Ricky Hatton
Homicide Hank / Hurricane Henry	Henry Armstrong
Hurricane	Rubin Carter
The Illinois Thunderbolt	Billy Papke

20TH-CENTURY TOP 10 BANTAMWEIGHTS

Rank	Boxer	Record (W–L–D)	KOs	Career
=1.	Ruben Olivares	88–13–3	78	1965–81
=1.	Carlos Zarate	61–4	58	1970–88
3.	Eder Jofre	72–2–4	50	1957–76
4.	Panama Al Brown	128–19–11, 4 ND	58	1922–42
5.	Manuel Ortiz	96–28–3	49	1938–55
=6.	Lionel Rose	42–11	12	1964–76
=6.	Fighting Harada	55–7	22	1960–70
8.	Alfonso Zamora	33–5	32	1973–80
9.	Sixto Escobar	45–22–3	30	1930–40
10.	Jimmy Carruthers	21–4	13	1950–62

Source: Associated Press, 30 December 1999

WHEN THE BOMBER WAS BOMBED

When Max Schmeling, the former world heavyweight champion (1930–32) entered the ring in New York on 19 June 1936 to face the awesome Joe Louis, the bookmakers had the German down as an 8–1 outsider to upset the "Brown Bomber". However, the 31-year-old Schmeling caused a major upset when he knocked his 22-year-old opponent to the floor in the fourth round. The knockdown gave Schmeling confidence and he eventually wore Louis down, with punch after punch hurting his opponent, and stopped him in round 12.

PHANTOM ROUND IS PHANTOM STORY

For almost 60 years, the story of Willie Pep's non-title fight against Jackie Graves in Minneapolis on 25 July 1946 included the amazing statistic that he won the third round of the fight despite the fact that he didn't throw a punch in the round. Pep won the fight with a TKO in round 8, but the legend of the third round was debunked in 2003.

BAER CALLS TIME IN THE RING

When Lou Nova stopped the former heavyweight champion of the world Max Baer (1934–5) in the eighth round of their bout in New York on 4 April 1941, Baer announced his retirement.

Did You Know That?
Baer fought Nova in the first televised heavyweight prizefight, on 1 June 1939 on WNBT-TV in New York.

⚜ FIGHTING TALK (15) ⚜

"Sure there have been injuries and deaths in boxing – but none of them serious."
Alan Minter

⚜ A BLACK DAY ALL ROUND ⚜

On 29 October 1929, Mickey Walker beat Ace Hudkins in 10 rounds to retain his world middleweight title on the same day that the famous Wall Street Stock Market Crash occurred. The market lost $14 billion in value on 29 October, to bring the total loss for the week to $30 billion, ten times more than the annual budget of the US government and more than the USA had spent in fighting the First World War.

⚜ THE CHOCOLATE KID ⚜

Kid Chocolate, born Eligio Sardinias Montalvo in Havana, Cuba, on 6 January 1910, knocked out Benny Bass in the seventh round of their world junior-lightweight championship fight in Philadelphia on 15 July 1931. However, four months later (on 20 November 1931) Tony Canzoneri beat Chocolate in 15 rounds in New York to retain the world lightweight and world junior-welterweight titles.

⚜ THE ROUND SQUARE ⚜

The earliest known Rules of Boxing were drawn up in Ancient Rome, where one of the rules required the two fighters to remain inside a circular ring drawn on the floor of the arena. Despite the transformation to square-shaped stages, they have been known as "rings" ever since.

⚜ BROWN BOMBER ENTERS THE RING ⚜

Joseph Louis Barrow, better known as Joe Louis (the "Brown Bomber"), made his professional debut in Chicago on 4 July 1934, and knocked out Jack Kracken in the first round.

⚜ KNOCKING OUT A TIGER ⚜

On 24 May 1968, Bob Foster knocked out Dick Tiger in round 4 of their bout in New York to win the world light-heavyweight title. It was the only KO suffered by Tiger in his entire professional career.

ONE-EYED MAX

During his heavyweight bout with Tommy Farr in New York on 11 March 1938, Max Baer sent his challenger to the floor in round 6, the first knockdown of Farr's career. Farr got back to his feet, but although Baer had to box most of the fight with one eye closed, he beat Farr in 15 rounds.

TUNNEY'S TITLE SHOT

On 5 June 1925, Gene Tunney knocked out Tommy Gibbons in 12 rounds in New York, which earned Tunney a shot at Jack Dempsey's world heavyweight title. It was a hard-fought victory against a man who had lasted 15 rounds with Dempsey and had never previously been knocked out.

NORTON BREAKS ALI'S JAW

Ken Norton faced the defending champion, Muhammad Ali, for the NABF heavyweight title in San Diego, California, on 31 March 1973. The hard-hitting challenger broke the champion's jaw en route to being crowned the new champion in 12 rounds. Seven months later, on 10 September 1973, Ali beat Norton in 12 rounds in Los Angeles to regain the NABF heavyweight belt. On 28 January 1974, Ali put his NABF heavyweight belt up against Joe Frazier in New York. The champion beat Smokin' Joe in 12 rounds to retain his title.

THE SHARK SAVAGES OPPONENT

On 12 October 1926, Harry Willis was on the receiving end of such a non-stop mauling by Jack Sharkey in Brooklyn, New York, that for most of the bout he tried to hold on to his attacker. In the 13th round the referee decided he had seen enough and disqualified the battered Willis for excessive holding.

LOUIS' TREBLE KO

When the reigning world heavyweight champion, Joe Louis, knocked out Jack Roper in the first round of their championship title bout in Los Angeles on 17 April 1939, it was the third consecutive time the "Brown Bomber" had retained his belt with a first-round KO. Louis' feat has never been equalled by a heavyweight, while the bout itself was the last heavyweight title fight scheduled for 10 rounds.

♔ WHEN THE WEIGHTS WERE UNFAIR ♚

On 16 October 1909, the reigning world middleweight champion, Stanley Ketchel, fought the reigning world heavyweight champion, Jack Johnson, in Colma, California, for Johnson's belt. The much lighter Ketchel floored Johnson in round 12, but the heavyweight Johnson got back up and battered Ketchel into submission to retain his crown.

Did You Know That?
When Johnson's gloves were removed Ketchel's two front teeth were found embedded in his right glove.

♔ TUNNEY'S ONLY DEFEAT ♚

Just over four months after Gene Tunney beat Battling Levinsky in 12 rounds in New York to win the American light-heavyweight title (13 January 1922), Harry Greb beat Tunney in 15 rounds in New York (23 May 1922) to strip the champion of his title and inflict the only defeat of Tunney's career. Tunney beat Greb in 15 rounds in New York on 23 February 1923 to regain the title. The pair met again on 10 December 1923, but the result of the fight was the same, with Tunney holding on to his belt.

♔ STANDING FIRM AGAINST THE ROCK ♚

When Ted Lowry lost to the future world heavyweight champion Rocky Marciano over 10 rounds in Providence, Rhode Island, on 13 November 1950, he claimed a remarkable boxing double. Lowry had also lasted 10 rounds against Marciano in October 1949 thereby giving him the honour of being the only fighter to go the distance twice with The Rock. Lowry's career record was 67 wins, 67 losses and 10 draws.

♔ LAST SCHEDULED 20-ROUNDER ♚

On 21 March 1941, Joe Louis knocked out Abe Simon in the 13th round of their world heavyweight title bout in Detroit to retain his belt. The fight was the last contest scheduled for 20 rounds.

♔ LAST 20-ROUNDER GOES THE DISTANCE ♚

When Max Baer beat King Levinsky in 20 rounds in Reno, Nevada, on 4 July 1932, their heavyweight fight was the last scheduled 20-round contest to go the full distance.

❦ SUGAR RAY LEONARD ❧

Raymond Charles "Sugar Ray" Leonard was born on 17 May 1956 in Wilmington, South Carolina. As soon as he pulled on his first pair of boxing gloves all he wanted to do was become a world champion. Sugar Ray won an amazing 145 of his 150 amateur fights, and ended his amateur career with the gold medal in the light-welterweight division of the 1976 Olympic Games in Montreal. After winning the gold medal Leonard said, "The journey is over, the dream fulfilled", and retired from boxing, stating that he wanted to go to college. However, with no endorsements, an illness to his father and the bills starting to pile up, Leonard returned to boxing, as a professional, and hired the legendary trainer, Angelo Dundee.

Leonard won his pro debut in February 1977, a unanimous six-round points verdict over Puerto Rico's Luis Vega. He was perfect in his next 24 contests to set up a match with WBC world welterweight champion Wilfred Benitez. The bout took place on 30 November 1979 in Las Vegas, with Leonard claiming the title with a final-round TKO. *Ring Magazine* named Sugar Ray the 1979 Fighter of the Year. In March 1980, he won his first defence, beating England's Dave "Boy" Green with a KO in round 4. Next up for Leonard was Roberto Duran, who defeated the champion on points over 15 rounds in Montreal on 20 June 1980, his first loss in 28 bouts. However, Sugar Ray reclaimed his belt in the rematch with Duran five months later.

On 25 June 1981, Leonard fought the undefeated WBA world light-middleweight champion, Ayub Kalule, in Houston and claimed his second world title with a ninth-round TKO. The fight the boxing public had been crying out for took place on 16 September 1981 when Sugar Ray faced the undefeated Thomas "Hitman" Hearns, the reigning WBA world welterweight champion at Caesar's Palace, Las Vegas. The unification bout was an out-and-out brawl with the advantage swaying both ways until the referee stopped the contest in round 14 in favour of Leonard.

After twice retiring, in 1982 and 1984, Leonard returned to fight WBC world middleweight champion, Marvelous Marvin Hagler, winning on points over 12 rounds at Caesar's Palace on 6 April 1987. Sugar Ray took the light-heavyweight title with a defeat of Donny Lalonde, but immediately vacated the crown. A draw with Hearns and a second defeat of Duran preceded a shock defeat against Terry Norris in February 1991. After six years out of the ring, and now at the age of 40, Leonard returned to fight Hector Camacho and the "Macho Man" became the only man ever to stop him. Sugar Ray retired for good with a professional career record of 36 wins, 3 losses and a draw.

⬗ YOUNG KNOCKOUT ⬗

On 3 July 1931, Max Schmeling knocked out Young Stribling in round 15 of their bout in Cleveland to retain his world heavyweight title. The KO was the first and the last suffered by Stribling in his 286-fight career.

⬗ WORLD CHAMP HITS THE MUSIC CHARTS ⬗

This Bike Is A Pipe Bomb, an American punk rock band from the Deep South, wrote a song in tribute to Jack Johnson, the legendary former world heavyweight boxing champion. Several hip-hop activists have also reflected on Johnson's legacy, most notably Mos Def, who released the single entitled "Blue Black Jack". Miles Davis and Wynton Marsalis both produced soundtracks for documentaries about Johnson's life.

⬗ LOUIS FOILS CONN MAN ⬗

Boxing fans cheered the long-awaited return to the ring of the world heavyweight champion, Joe Louis, when he faced Billy Conn in the Bronx, New York, on 19 June 1946. It was the champ's first fight in four years, and he did not let his army of fans down, knocking out Conn in round 8 of the bout to retain his heavyweight belt.

⬗ NOT ALL WRIGHT ON THE NIGHT ⬗

On 4 December 1999, Fernando Vargas and Ronald "Winky" Wright met in the last world championship fight of the twentieth century. The pair met in Lincoln City, Oregon, with Vargas placing his IBF world light-middleweight belt on the line. The champion had to come from behind to take a 12-round points decision and retain his title.

⬗ MIND GAME ⬗

Prior to a bout between Benny Leonard and Richie Mitchell, the referee explained the then newly introduced rule that after a boxer knocks his opponent to the canvas that boxer must retire to a neutral corner. At this Leonard looked at the referee and said: "Let me get this straight. As I understand it, every time I knock him down I'm to go to a neutral corner?" Leonard's remark unsettled his opponent, and although Mitchell sent Leonard to the floor in the opening round, Leonard knocked Mitchell out in the sixth.

❧ CHAMP ON THE RUN ❧

On 19 December 1913, the reigning world heavyweight champion Jack Johnson retained his title despite suffering a broken left arm in his 10-round draw with challenger Battling Jim Johnson in Paris, France. Jack Johnson was forced to fight abroad having fled the USA on 1 July 1913 after receiving a one-year prison sentence.

Did You Know That?
The Johnson v. Johnson fight was the first world heavyweight title fight in which both boxers were African-American.

❧ DOWN BUT FAR FROM OUT ❧

On 22 February 1910, Battling Nelson looked on course to retain his world lightweight title when he sent his opponent, Ad Wolgast, crashing to the canvas in round 23 of their bout in Point Richmond, California. However, the challenger survived the knockdown and went on to claim the title in the 40th round.

❧ THE DOUBLE KNOCKOUT ❧

On 4 July 1912, boxing's most famous double knockout occurred when the reigning world lightweight champion Ad Wolgast looked to be out cold after Joe Rivers caught him with a devastating punch. However, with the assistance of the referee the champion managed to stay on his feet and knocked his opponent out in round 13 to retain his belt in Vernon, California.

❧ NO MERCY SHOWN ❧

On 25 February 1918, Jack Dempsey sent Bill Brennan crashing to the canvas eight times before stopping him in round 6 in Milwaukee. One of the falls resulted in Brennan suffering a broken ankle.

❧ REFEREE GETS A CRACK AT THE TITLE ❧

On 27 June 1914, Jack Johnson, still a fugitive from justice in the USA, beat Frank Moran in Paris to retain his world heavyweight title. The referee for the contest was the reigning European heavyweight champion Georges Carpentier, who thus gained the unique distinction of officiating in a world heavyweight championship bout seven years before fighting for the same title himself.

☙ FIGHTING TALK (16) ☙

"Joe Frazier is so ugly, he should donate his face to the US Bureau of Wildlife."
Muhammad Ali

☙ GRAZIANO BANNED ☙

On 7 February 1947, the New York State Athletic Commission (NYSAC) revoked the former world welterweight champion Rocky Graziano's licence to fight in New York, and threatened to bar him from boxing for life, after Rocky failed to notify the NYSAC of two six-figure offers to throw a fight. Graziano was subsequently permitted to box in any other US State and reclaimed the middleweight title in his very next bout, held in Chicago, Illinois. The world champion was later reinstated by the NYSAC.

☙ ROCKY THE UNDERDOG ☙

Rocky Graziano went into his fight with Billy Arnold in New York on 9 March 1945 as a 7–1 underdog with the bookies. Arnold was giving Rocky a boxing lesson in the first two rounds before Rocky let loose and stopped his opponent in round 3. Just over three months later, on 29 June 1945, Graziano was trailing reigning world welterweight champion Freddie "Red" Cochrane after nine rounds and then knocked out the champ. Graziano and Cochrane had a rematch on 24 August 1945 in New York, and after falling behind on points once again Rocky stopped Red in 10 rounds.

☙ SAVED BY THE BELL ☙

On 3 July 1905, the former light-heavyweight champion Jack Root landed a punch on the chin of Marvin Hart that sent his opponent crashing to the canvas in Reno, Nevada. Had the bell not rung seconds after he hit the floor, Hart would have been counted out. Five rounds later a revived Hart knocked out Root to claim the vacant world heavyweight title.

☙ ST PATRICK'S DAY ENDS LONG FIGHTS ☙

Bobby McIntyre's bout with Bobby Ruffin, in New Orleans on 17 March 1943, in which McIntyre scored a 17th-round knockout win, was the last fight to go more than 15 rounds of boxing.

⚜ A DRAMATIC ROUND OF BOXING ⚜

In a world lightweight title fight in New York on 14 January 1921, Benny Leonard sent his opponent Richie Mitchell to the floor three times, and was then sent crashing to the canvas and almost knocked out himself in one of the most dramatic rounds of boxing ever witnessed. Eventually Leonard knocked Mitchell out in round 6 of their bout to retain his title.

⚜ BOXING'S MOST PROLIFIC FIGHTER ⚜

Leonard Wickwar was born on 11 March 1911 in Leicester, England. He turned professional in 1928, and in 1933 he became the featherweight champion of the Midlands, for which he received the sum of £100 and the famous "Ted Salmon's Gold Championship Belt" (which was subsequently stolen from a Leicester pub where it was on display). He fought his final bout on 6 February 1947, losing to Danny Cunningham at St James's Hill, Newcastle-upon-Tyne. Wickwar is widely considered to be the most prolific boxer in history, having fought 465 bouts, and holds the record both for the most wins (337) and the most losses (128) by any fighter.

⚜ WHEN THE ROCK NEARLY CRUMBLED ⚜

Just when it looked like someone would finally beat Rocky Marciano, the world heavyweight champion landed one of his famous trademark punches to the jaw to knock out his opponent. Jersey Joe Walcott had sent the champion crashing to the canvas in the opening round of their bout in Philadelphia on 23 September 1952, and he went on battering the champ during the fight, inflicting cuts over both eyes and on his head, before Rocky landed his thunderous right in round 13 to retain his heavyweight title.

⚜ SUGAR RUNS LOW ⚜

Sugar Ray Robinson, the reigning world middleweight champion, attempted to reclaim the world lightweight title when he faced Joey Maxim in New York on 25 June 1952. However, on a sultry evening the former champion succumbed to dehydration and heat exhaustion and dropped to the canvas in round 13. When he was unable to come out for round 14 the referee awarded the bout to the defending champion. Robinson's loss was the only time in his 26-year career that he was unable to finish a fight.

⚜ A CENTURY OF FIGHTS – 1980–89 ⚜

20 Jun 80 Roberto Duran beat Sugar Ray Leonard in 15 rounds in Montreal to claim the WBC world welterweight crown.

11 May 81 By stopping Ken Norton in the opening round of their bout in New York, Gerry Cooney caused the biggest upset in the ring since Leon Spinks took Muhammad Ali's world heavyweight title in 1978.

13 Nov 82 Ray "Boom Boom" Mancini stopped Duk-Koo Kim in 14 rounds in Las Vegas to retain his WBA world lightweight title. Sadly Kim lapsed into a coma and died five days later.

27 May 83 "Marvelous" Marvin Hagler and Wilford Scypion made boxing history when they fought in Providence, Rhode Island. Hagler knocked out Scypion in round 4 to retain his world middleweight title. The fight was the first title bout sanctioned by the USBA/International, which later became the International Boxing Federation (IBF).

1 Dec 84 Greg Page knocked out Gerrie Coetzee in eight rounds in Sun City, South Africa, to win the WBA world heavyweight title.

7 Jul 85 Julio Cesar Chavez stopped Roger Mayweather in two rounds in Las Vegas to retain his WBC world junior-lightweight title.

12 Jul 86 Evander Holyfield outpointed Dwight Muhammad Qawi in Atlanta to win the WBA world cruiserweight title.

9 Mar 87 George Foreman ended a 10-year retirement from boxing when he stopped Steve Zouski in round 4 of their heavyweight bout in Sacramento, California.

7 Nov 88 Sugar Ray Leonard knocked out Donny Lalonde in the ninth round in Las Vegas to claim the WBC world super-middleweight and world light-heavyweight belts.

24 Feb 89 Roberto Duran beat Iran Barkley in 12 rounds in Atlantic City to win the WBC world middleweight title, his fourth division title. Barkley, nicknamed "The Blade", had sensationally won the belt from Thomas "Hitman" Hearns on 6 June 1988.

⚜ TAKE ME TO THE ROOF ⚜

After Joe Louis knocked out Eddie Simms in the opening round of their bout in Cleveland, Ohio, on 14 December 1936, Simms is reported to have said to the referee, "Take me up to the roof, I need to get some air." The fight lasted a mere 14 seconds.

ॐ 20TH-CENTURY TOP 10 FLYWEIGHTS ॐ

Rank	Boxer	Record (W–L–D)	KOs	Career
=1.	Pancho Villa	76–5–5, 21 ND	23	1919–25
=1.	Miguel Canto	61–9–4	15	1969–82
3.	Jimmy Wilde	131–3–2, 13 ND	99	1910–23
4.	Fidel La Barba	75–15–8, 1 ND	17	1924–33
5.	Frankie Genaro	82–21–8, 19 ND	19	1920–34
6.	Small Montana	79–22–10	10	1931–41
7.	Charchai Chionoi	63–19–3	39	1957–75
8.	Ricardo Lopez	51–0–1	38	1985–2001
=9.	Corporal Izzy Schwartz	58–27–12	5	1922–32
=9.	Jackie Patterson	64–25–3	41	1938–51

* = Active in 1999 (record at 1 June 2009)   Source: Associated Press, 30 December 1999

ॐ YANKEE STADIUM'S LAST TITLE FIGHT ॐ

Muhammad Ali beat Ken Norton in 15 rounds at Yankee Stadium, New York, on 28 September 1976 to retain his world heavyweight title. It was the last ever title fight held in Yankee Stadium.

ॐ TURNAROUND IN FORTUNES ॐ

Donald Curry was giving the reigning WBA world junior-middleweight champion, Mike McCallum, a boxing lesson in the first rounds of their bout in Las Vegas on 18 July 1987, and was well ahead on the judges' scorecards. Then, in round 5, the champion landed a beautifully timed left hook square on the challenger's jaw to knock him out and retain his belt.

ॐ BLACK IS BEAUTIFUL ॐ

On Boxing Day 1908, Jack Johnson became the first African-American to win the world heavyweight title when he stopped the much-travelled defending champion, Canadian-born Tommy Burns, in the 14th round of their title fight at Rushcutter's Bay, Sydney, Australia.

ॐ CHAMPIONS IN THE MAKING ॐ

On 26 September 1959, Benny "Kid" Paret drew a 10-round contest in San Juan with Jose Torres. Paret would go on to be crowned the world welterweight champion, while Torres went on to be crowned world light-heavyweight champion.

✑ THE JAPANESE FIGHTING MACHINE ✑

In October 1962, the 19-year-old Masahiko "Fighting" Harada won the world flyweight championship belt, beating Pone Kingpetch, but lost it to the same opponent in January 1963. He then moved up the weight divisions and defeated Eder Jofre to claim the world bantamweight title on 17 May 1965 in Nagoya, Japan. In 1968 Harada lost his bantamweight crown to Lionel Rose, and after two unsuccessful attempts to land the WBC featherweight title he retired in 1970.

✑ CHOCOLATE MELTS UNDER THE LIGHTS ✑

On 24 November 1933, in the second round of their second fight, in New York, Tony Canzoneri knocked out Kid Chocolate. It was the first KO defeat for the Kid and it came in his 97th pro fight.

✑ COURAGE KNOWS NO LIMIT ✑

South African boxer Courage Tshabalala, nicknamed "No Limit", began his professional career in 1993 after a hugely successful amateur career with 72 wins, 1 loss and 69 first-round knockouts. The big heavyweight won his first 19 pro fights and looked set for the big time until Brian Scott beat him by TKO in 1996. He lost his next bout by TKO to Darroll Wilson in 1997, and after being knocked out by Oleg Maskaev, the future WBC world champion, in Russia in 1998, he retired. Tshabalala made a brief return to the ring in 2003 and won his first three fights before being TKO'd by Robert Wiggins, after which he retired for good.

✑ SWEDISH CONTROVERSY ✑

On 14 September 1968, Jimmy Ellis was awarded a controversial 15-round victory over Floyd Patterson in Stockholm, Sweden, to retain his WBA world heavyweight title.

✑ GOLDEN GLOVES TOURNAMENT ✑

In 1923 the sports editor of the *Chicago Tribune*, a man named Arch Ward, founded a boxing tournament which he hoped would help to keep young people busy and to promote the sport at amateur level. He named his tournament "Golden Gloves", and the winner of each division was to receive a small golden boxing glove.

❧ THE FIGHTING JAPANESE ❧

The first world title bout between two Japanese fighters took place on 14 December 1967 in Tokyo. Hiroshi Kobayashi met Yoshiaki Numata in the ring for the WBA and WBC world super-featherweight title, and Kobayashi became the undisputed champion of the world after knocking out his opponent in round 12. However, Kobayashi was stripped of his WBA belt when he declined to fight Rene Barrientos. He defended the WBC title six times before losing it to Alfredo Marcano in 1971. Later that year he retired after being knocked out in the seventh round of his fight with a young Roberto Duran.

❧ ST VALENTINE'S DAY MASSACRE ❧

In Chicago on 14 February 1951, Sugar Ray Robinson gave Jake LaMotta a terrible beating before finally stopping his brave challenger in round 13 to win the world welterweight championship. It was the sixth and final time the pair met in the ring.

❧ BOTH FIGHTERS SUSPENDED ❧

So many fouls were committed in the world featherweight title bout in New York between Sandy Saddler and Willie Pep, on 26 September 1951, that after the fight the New York State Athletic Commission suspended both fighters. The contest ended with Saddler retaining his belt after Pep did not get off his stool for round 10.

❧ ROUND 50 AND IT'S ALL OVER ❧

The longest fight of the twentieth century took place in Paris, France, on 17 April 1909, when Joe Jeannette and Sam McVey met in a bruising heavyweight encounter. Jeannette was declared the winner when McVey could not summon up the energy to come out for round 50.

❧ A BUSY MONTH ❧

On 14 October 1921, Ted "Kid" Lewis knocked out Johnny Basham in 12 rounds in London to retain his British middleweight championship and also claim the European middleweight crown. Then, on 17 November 1921, Lewis knocked out Noel McCormick in the 14th round to claim the British light-heavyweight title.

✥ THE FAB FOUR: HAGLER V. HEARNS ✥

On 15 April 1985, boxing fans were treated to the sixth instalment of the Fab Four's meetings when the 5ft 9½in Marvin Hagler, unbeaten since 1976, put his middleweight title on the line against the 6ft 1in tall Thomas Hearns at Caesar's Palace in Las Vegas. Hagler had been criticized in the press for not stopping Duran inside 15 rounds, and from the opening bell of the bout he rushed at Hearns, throwing everything he could at his challenger. Hearns responded ferociously, landing punch after punch on Hagler and leaving the champion badly cut. At the end of the second round the ring doctor was asked by the referee to look at Hagler's cuts, but thanks to the skilful and expert work of his cuts man Hagler was allowed to fight on. Hearns pushed forward in round 3, the round in which he had predicted a knockout, but the bloodied champion fought back and stunned both Hearns and the audience when he knocked his challenger out. Hagler hit Hearns so hard that it took Hearns a few minutes to leave the ring, and he had to be carried to the dressing-room by his cornermen. The crowd witnessed a brief but classic toe-to-toe slug fest that night between two magnificent fighters, both in their prime. After the fight the shaven-headed Hagler, who always looked a menacing sight, said: "There's only one way to fight Thomas Hearns. I cut Thomas Hearns down like a tree."

✥ A GOOD YEAR FOR CHAMPIONS ✥

Two legendary boxers and future world heavyweight champions were born in 1906. On 7 June, James J. Braddock was born in New York City, and on 26 October Primo Carnera was born in Sequals, Italy.

✥ FRAZIER TOO QUICK IN THE MOTOR CITY ✥

Joe Frazier knocked out the defending world light-heavyweight champion Bob Foster in round 2 of their bout in Detroit, Michigan on 18 November 1970 to retain his belt.

✥ RECORD 11 TITLE DEFENCES IN ONE YEAR ✥

The defending world welterweight champion Henry Armstrong knocked out Jimmy Garrison in the seventh round of their title fight in Cleveland on 11 December 1939. It was the 11th time the champion had defended his welterweight title in 1939, a record for any weight class during one year that has never been equalled.

⚜ FIGHTING TALK (17) ⚜

"Yeah, I'm scared. I'm scared I might kill Schmeling."
Joe Louis

⚜ WE'LL MEET AGAIN ⚜

On 26 March 1915, Jack Britton and Ted "Kid" Lewis fought over 10 rounds in New York before the judges declared the fight a no decision. It was the first of a scheduled 20-fight series between the pair. On 21 June 1915, Britton beat Mike Glover in 12 rounds in Boston to claim the world welterweight title. Two months later, on 31 August, Britton lost the title when defeated by Lewis in 12 rounds in Boston.

⚜ A RECORD KO ⚜

On 1 September 1908, the reigning world heavyweight champion Tommy Burns knocked out Bill Lang in the sixth round of their title fight in Melbourne, Australia. It was Burns's eighth consecutive knockout in the defence of his heavyweight crown, a record Larry Holmes equalled in 1981 and which still stands today.

Did You Know That?
In December 1908, Burns became the first fighter to agree to fight a black boxer for the world heavyweight championship. He lost to Jack Johnson in Australia.

⚜ THE BATTLING CHAMPION ⚜

On 4 July 1908, Battling Nelson knocked out Joe Gans in the 17th round of their world lightweight championship fight in Colma, California. On 26 November 1910, Freddie Welsh floored Nelson five times in the 11th round of their fight in San Francisco, California, the fifth knockdown resulting in the only 10-count of Nelson's career.

⚜ A VALUABLE LESSON ⚜

On 25 November 1905, Joe Jeanette beat Jack Johnson on a foul in the second round of their heavyweight fight in Philadelphia. Subsequently Johnson never lost another fight until 1915, a run that included a victory over 15 rounds in his next fight against Jeanette in Baltimore on 14 March 1906.

SOVIET SUPREMACY

Boxers from the old Soviet Union have enjoyed much success since it broke up in the late twentieth century. The following have been world heavyweight champions and were born in the former USSR:

Name	State born
Ruslan Chagaev	Uzbekistan
Sultan Ibragimov	Russia
Wladimir Klitschko	Kazakhstan
Vitali Klitschko	Kyrgyzstan
Sergei Liakhovich	Belarus
Oleg Maskaev	Kazakhstan
Nikolai Valuev	Russia
Alexander Povetkin	Russia

EX-CON MAKES HEAVY MOVES

In the early 1970s the biggest names on the heavyweight fight scene were Muhammad Ali, George Foreman and Joe Frazier. However, making his way up the rankings was a fighter who knocked out rivals as regularly as Foreman and who had previously spent more than seven years in the Colorado State Penitentiary. The fighter in question was Ron Lyle, who after being released from prison in November 1969 had many bruising battles against the best heavyweight contenders of the era. However, Lyle never won the world heavyweight championship, although he was given a crack at Muhammad Ali's WBA and WBC belts on 16 May 1975 in Las Vegas, Nevada. It was Ali's second defence of the belts he won by knocking out Foreman in the "Rumble in the Jungle" (his first defence was a TKO against Chuck Wepner). Going into round 11, Lyle was well ahead on the judge's scorecards, but Ali's "rope-a-dope" tactics instantly paid dividends for the champion when he exploded with a perfect combination. The referee stopped the bout, awarding Ali a TKO, at which Lyle and his manager went crazy, believing the bout should have been allowed to continue. However, the referee's decision was justified, as Lyle could barely defend himself, let alone hit Ali.

DEMPSEY'S SHOW

When Paulino Uzcudun beat Max Baer in 20 rounds in Reno, Nevada, on 4 July 1931, the promoter and referee for the contest was the former world heavyweight champion, Jack Dempsey.

KING OF THE BANTAMWEIGHTS

When the reigning world bantamweight champion Manuel Ortiz defeated Benny Goldberg in 15 rounds in Los Angeles on 23 November 1943, it was the eighth time he successfully defended his belt at the weight, a record in the division.

FOSTER CALLS IT A DAY

Three months after Bob Foster drew with Jorge Ahumada in Albuquerque, New Mexico (the fight took place on 17 July 1974) to retain his world light-heavyweight title, Foster announced his retirement from the sport.

HOLYFIELD CRUISES TO VICTORY

On 15 May 1987, WBA world cruiserweight champion Evander Holyfield stopped Rickey Parkey in three rounds in Las Vegas, Nevada to claim his IBF cruiserweight title. Then, on 9 April 1988, Holyfield stopped WBC champion Carlos De Leon in Las Vegas to unify the cruiserweight division.

NO SHOW FOR TEOFILO

In the lead-up to the 1984 Olympic Games in Los Angeles, the world of boxing looked forward to seeing the legendary Cuban boxer Teofilo Stevenson attempt to win a record fourth consecutive heavyweight gold medal. However, when the Soviet Union boycotted the Games, in retaliation for the USA boycott of the 1980 Moscow Olympics, communist Cuba followed the Soviets' lead, and his chance was gone.

THE START OF SOMETHING GREAT

During the 1960 Olympic Games in Rome, 18-year-old Cassius Marcellus Clay, later known as Muhammad Ali, won the gold medal in boxing's light-heavyweight division, defeating Poland's Zbigniew Pietryskowsky in the final. Ali would go on to become the undisputed heavyweight boxing champion of the world and one of the greatest sporting icons of the twentieth century.

Did You Know That?
The young Clay was so proud of his gold medal that he kept it on for two days.

⬡ HOMICIDE HANK ⬡

On 29 October 1937, in New York, Henry Armstrong (who was born Henry Jackson on 12 December 1912) knocked out Petey Sarron in the sixth round to claim the world featherweight championship. Just 44 days later in New Orleans (12 December 1937) Armstrong, nicknamed "Homicide Hank", then knocked out Johnny Jones in round 2 of their bout to end the year with an unblemished 27–0 record, 26 of his 27 wins in 1937 by way of knockout. On 31 May 1938, Armstrong as reigning world featherweight champion beat Barney Ross in Long Island to win the world welterweight championship. The sporting Armstrong, who was simply too good for his opponent, actually took it easy on Ross over the final rounds of their bout so that the old champion could go out maintaining his proud record of never having been stopped in a fight. Then on 17 August 1938, Armstrong claimed a 15-round split decision win over Lou Ambers to win the world lightweight title. His defeat of Ambers gave him the unique distinction of being the only boxer in history to hold three world championship belts at different weights at the same time – featherweight, lightweight and welterweight. Armstrong defended the world welterweight belt more times than any other fighter and ended his career with a record of 151 wins (101 KOs), 21 losses and 9 draws, although his actual fight record is unclear as some boxing historians believe Armstrong fought some pay fights under the alias of Melody Jackson. In 2002 Armstrong was rated second only to the legendary Sugar Ray Leonard in *Ring Magazine*'s list of the "Greatest Fighters of the Last 80 Years".

Did You Know That?
Armstrong was a cousin of the legendary American jazz singer Billie Holiday.

⬡ THE GHETTO WIZARD ⬡

On 15 January 1925, Benny Leonard retired as the undefeated world lightweight champion, aged just 28. Leonard had a rough upbringing in a Jewish ghetto on the east side of Manhattan, in New York, and because he learned how to fight on the streets he was nicknamed the "Ghetto Wizard". During his career (which included an ill-advised comeback in 1931) Leonard won 157 fights (69 KOs), lost 11, drew 5 and had 40 no contests. He fought his final fight on 7 October 1932 in which he was TKO'd in round 6 by the future world welterweight champion, Jimmy McLarnin.

✦ CHAMP ROUGHED UP ✦

In the first round of their heavyweight clash in Washington on 23 May 1941, Buddy Baer (Max Baer's younger brother) knocked the reigning world heavyweight champion Joe Louis out of the ring. However, the roughed-up champ climbed back into the ring and gradually worked his way back into the brawl and floored his challenger three times in round 6, the last knockdown coming after the bell had sounded. Baer's manager, Ancil Hoffman, was so incensed by the late punch that he refused to allow his fighter to appear for round 7. As a result the referee disqualified Baer and awarded the bout to Louis, making it the 17th consecutive successful defence of his belt. The pair met again in a rematch on 9 January 1942 at Madison Square Garden, New York, with the champion once again retaining his title (it was his 20th consecutive successful defence) and this time knocking out Baer in the opening round. Speaking some time later about their rematch Baer said: "The only way I could have beaten Louis that night was with a baseball bat."

✦ FAIRYTALE COMES TO AN END ✦

On 22 June 1937, James J. Braddock (nicknamed the "Cinderella Man") lost his world heavyweight championship belt to Joe Louis in Chicago. Despite sending his opponent crashing to the floor in the opening round, the champion was no match for Louis' all-out aggressive style and was knocked out by his challenger in the eighth round. Louis only got his shot at the title when negotiations between Madison Square Garden and Max Schmeling, who beat Louis a few months earlier to become the No.1 contender, broke down. Braddock opted for the bigger payday against Louis. Following his win the newly crowned champion said: "I won't feel like I'm the champ until I whip Schmeling." On 22 June 1938, Louis retained his title against Schmeling when the referee stopped the bout with just 2 minutes and 4 seconds of the first round gone. Shortly after the opening bell sounded Louis unintentionally punched Schmeling in the lower back when his challenger attempted to turn away from a punch (Schmeling later claimed that it was an illegal punch to the kidney). However, the blow fractured two of the German's vertebrae leaving him writhing in pain before Louis landed another crushing blow which sent the former champion to the floor. When Louis put Schmeling down two more times the referee ended the bout and afterwards said he stopped it so early "to keep Schmeling from being killed". After the fight a delighted Louis told reporters: "Now you can call me champ."

❦ FIGHTING TALK (18) ❧

"You always say, 'I'll quit when I start to slide', and then one morning you wake up and realize you done slid."
Sugar Ray Robinson

❦ ALL OVER FOR MONZON ❧

On 30 July 1977, Carlos Monzon was sent to the canvas by Rodrigo Valdes in round 2 of their world middleweight championship bout in Monte Carlo, but the defending champion got to his feet and retained his belt in 15 rounds. Thirty days later, on 29 August 1977, Monzon retired aged 35.

❦ NO APRIL FOOL ❧

On 1 April 1961, Emile Griffith knocked out Benny "Kid" Paret in round 13 of their fight in Miami Beach to claim the world welterweight title. Eight months later, on 9 December 1961, Gene Fullmer stopped Paret in 10 rounds in Las Vegas to retain his NBA middleweight belt.

❦ ROCKY THROWS IN THE TOWEL ❧

Rocky Graziano brought the curtain down on his boxing career in Chicago on 17 September 1952 following his loss to Chuck Davey in 10 rounds. Davey went on to challenge Kid Gavilan for his world welterweight title, but was knocked out in the 10th round on 11 February 1953 in Chicago.

❦ THE FAMILY BUSINESS ❧

Cory Spinks, the son of former world heavyweight champion Leon Spinks, and nephew of ex-world champ Michael Spinks, has upheld the family tradition. He was the undisputed world welterweight champion and also held the IBF light-middleweight title.

❦ BUDDY'S ST VALENTINE'S DAY JOY ❧

Buddy McGirt stopped Frankie Warren in 12 rounds in Corpus Christi, Texas, to win the vacant IBF world junior welterweight title on 14 February 1988. On 3 September that year, McGirt lost his belt to Meldrick Taylor, who stopped him, again in the 12th, in Atlantic City.

❧ THERE'S ONLY ONE JOSE ☙

John H. Stracey stopped Jose Napoles in six rounds in Mexico City on 6 December 1975 to win the world welterweight title in what proved to be the last fight of Napoles's distinguished career.

❧ SOUTH AMERICAN BIG HITTERS ☙

On 10 June 1960, Eder Jofre knocked out Ernesto Miranda in round 3 of their bout in Sao Paolo to retain his South American bantamweight title. Five months later, on 18 November 1960, Jofre knocked out Eloy Sanchez in the sixth round of their bout in Los Angeles to win the world bantamweight title.

❧ WHAT A RECORD ☙

Great Britain's Hal Bagwell holds the record for the greatest number of bouts without defeat during his entire career. In his 10 years as a professional (10 August 1938 to 29 November 1948), Bagwell racked up the almost perfect record of 175 wins, 0 losses, 2 draws and 3 no decisions.

❧ MAXIM POWER ☙

Very few boxing commentators gave the former light-heavyweight champion, Joey Maxim, much chance of defeating the 19-year-old Floyd Patterson when the pair met in the ring in Brooklyn, New York on 7 June 1954. However, Maxim handed the up-and-coming Patterson the first defeat of his career, claiming an eight-round decision.

❧ CHAMP DOWN UNDER ☙

On 27 December 1909, Bill Lang knocked out 46-year-old Bob Fitzsimmons in the 12th round of their fight in Sydney to retain his Australian heavyweight title. The ageing Fitzsimmons had been on top for most of the contest before running out of steam.

❧ THE LAST EVER BARE-KNUCKLE FIGHT ☙

On 7 September 1902, Bill Squires knocked out Peter Mills in the second round of their bare-knuckle fight in Narrabi, Australia. The fight is the last recorded bare-knuckle contest under London Prize Ring Rules.

⚞ A CENTURY OF FIGHTS – 1990–99 ⚟

25 Oct 90 Eight months after James "Buster" Douglas caused one of the most sensational upsets in boxing history when he defeated the previously unbeaten Mike Tyson in Tokyo to claim the world heavyweight crown, Evander Holyfield knocked out the new world champion in Las Vegas to win the heavyweight title.

15 Mar 91 Two world lightweight champions stepped into the ring for a much anticipated showdown in Sacramento, California. The judges couldn't separate IBC title-holder, Tony Lopez, and WBA champion, Brian Mitchell, so the bout was called a draw after 12 rounds.

15 May 92 In the opening round of their bout for the vacant WBO world heavyweight title, both Michael Moorer and Bert Cooper found themselves on the floor. After Moorer got off the deck for a second time in round 3, he stopped Cooper in round 5 to claim the belt.

18 Dec 93 Simon Brown caused a shock when he knocked out Terry Norris in round 4 of their bout in Mexico to win the WBC world junior-middleweight title.

29 Jan 94 Julio Cesar Chavez suffered both the first knockdown of his professional career and his first defeat when Frankie Randall claimed a 12-round decision in Las Vegas to become the new WBC world junior-welterweight champion.

11 Mar 95 Riddick Bowe stopped Herbie Hide in six rounds to win the WBO world heavyweight title.

23 Mar 96 Arturo Gatti staged one of the greatest ever comebacks in boxing when he put his IBF world junior-lightweight belt up against Wilson Rodriguez. For five rounds the challenger battered the champion mercilessly, sending him to the canvas and almost closing both his eyes through swelling. Amazingly, Gatti knocked out his opponent in round 6 to retain his title.

4 Oct 97 Lennox Lewis retained his WBC world heavyweight title with a first-round stoppage of Poland's Andrew Golota in Atlantic City, New Jersey.

28 Aug 98 William Joppy stopped Robert Duran in round 3 in Las Vegas to retain his WBA world middleweight title.

18 Sep 99 Felix Trinidad outpointed Oscar De La Hoya over 12 rounds in Las Vegas to unify the IBF and WBC world welterweight belts.

∞ JOE CALZAGHE ∞

Joe Calzaghe has strong claims to be called Britain's greatest ever boxer. Although born in London on 23 March 1972 (to an Italian father, Enzo, and Welsh mother, Jackie), the family moved to Wales in 1974, and Joe considers himself Welsh. Enzo encouraged him to take up boxing at the age of nine, after he was bullied at school. He quickly impressed and won three British schoolboy titles. In 1993 Joe won the Amateur Boxing Association middleweight title, having been light-middleweight champion in 1992 and won the welterweight crown a year earlier.

In September 1993, Joe signed to the Mickey Duff/Terry Lawless boxing stable and made his professional debut the following month on the under-card at the Mike Tyson v. Frank Bruno world title fight at Cardiff Arms Park. He stopped Paul Hanlon in the opening round. Over the next four years, he fought 20 more opponents and only one – Bobbie Joe Edwards – went the distance. In 1995 Joe stopped Peter Wilson in eight rounds to win the British super-middleweight title and was voted Young Boxer of the Year by both the Professional Boxing Association and the Boxing Writers' Club.

After signing with Frank Warren, Joe earned his first world title shot. On 11 October 1997, he met Chris Eubank at the Sheffield Arena for the vacant WBO world super-middleweight crown. He knocked down the former multiple world title-holder in the opening round and won a unanimous points decision. When the undefeated Jeff Lacy put his IBF title on the line for a unification bout at the MEN Arena in Manchester on 5 March 2006, he lost by 14, 12 and 12 points, this despite Calzaghe, who landed more than 1,000 punches, having a point deducted.

Having given up the IBF crown early in 2007, Joe fought and crushed Peter Manfredo Jr. with only the WBO title at stake. Seven months, later, on 3 November 2007, Calzaghe faced WBA and WBC title-holder Mikkel Kessler of Denmark at the Millennium Stadium, Cardiff. He unified the title with a unanimous points decision. One reward for this victory was the BBC Sports Personality of the Year Award for 2007. With no opponents to conquer at super-middleweight, Joe stepped up to 173 pounds in 2008 and won points decisions over two ring legends, Bernard Hopkins and Roy Jones Jr. In February 2009, now 36 and the longest reigning title-holder in boxing history, Calzaghe announced his retirement, boasting a perfect 46–0 record, 32 inside the distance, and a guaranteed place in the pantheon of British boxing greats.

Did You Know That?
Joe Calzaghe suffered only one loss in 117 bouts as an amateur – a contest refereed by his opponent's father.

❧ BOXING'S KNIGHTS ❧

Only two men best known for their boxing exploits have ever received knighthoods. The first was Sir Dan Donnelly, the champion of Ireland, around 1819, and the second was Sir Henry Cooper, who received his honour in 2000. There are a couple of different accounts of how the young Donnelly got involved with boxing, with perhaps the most romantic being that he came to the aid of his elderly father who was being bullied by a huge sailor in a bar. It is said that word soon spread about the boy's bravery, which so infuriated a local champion boxer that he issued Donnelly with a challenge to fight him for his title. Donnelly did not wish to fight but reluctantly accepted and knocked out the Irish champion in the 16th round. Donnelly fought his last ever bout on 21 July 1819 at Crawley Downs, Sussex, against the man nicknamed the "Battersea Gardener", Tom Oliver. Legend has it that, after he knocked out Oliver with a stunning right hook in round 34, he was subsequently knighted by the Prince Regent (later King George IV) – who may have had money on him.

❧ FASTEST EVER HEAVYWEIGHT CHAMPION ❧

Leon Spinks, born in St. Louis, Missouri, on 11 July 1953, caused one of the most stunning upsets in the history of professional sport on 15 February 1978 when he beat the reigning world heavyweight champion, Muhammad Ali, in 15 rounds in Las Vegas to claim the WBA and WBC titles. Spinks, who had won the gold medal in the light-heavyweight division at the 1976 Olympic Games in Montreal, went into the fight as a 10–1 underdog and was only making his eighth professional appearance. In defeating Ali, Spinks became the fastest man ever to win the world heavyweight title, having notched up six wins and one draw prior to meeting Ali. Exactly seven months later, in New Orleans, Ali regained the WBA title – Spinks had been stripped of the WBC version – with a unanimous points verdict.

❧ DURAN KO'S A HORSE ❧

There is a famous story that Roberto "Hands of Stone" Duran once knocked out a horse with a punch. In another story, after Duran knocked out Pedro Mendoza in the opening round of their bout in Managua, Nicaragua in 1975, Mendoza's girlfriend/wife climbed into the ring and verbally abused Duran until, having heard enough insults, he decked her.

⚜ THE ALI–SPINKS MATCH-UPS ⚜

After losing his WBA and WBC world heavyweight titles to
Leon Spinks in Las Vegas, Nevada, on 15 February 1978 by way
of split decision, Muhammad Ali then reclaimed the WBA belt,
defeating Spinks in New Orleans, Louisiana, on 15 September 1978
by unanimous decision. After his win over Ali, Spinks had been
required to fight the mandatory challenger Ken Norton for his WBC
title, but elected instead to step into the ring with Ali for a rematch.
The WBC stripped Spinks of their belt on 18 March 1978 and
presented it to Norton without him having to fight to win it.

Did You Know That?
In his first defence of the WBC title, Norton faced the WBC's new
No. 1 contender Larry Holmes, losing their 15-round bout by a split
decision. The September 1998 edition of *Ring Magazine* listed the
final round of the Norton v. Holmes bout as one of the "12 Greatest
Finishes of All Time".

⚜ THE UNBEATABLE ROCK ⚜

World heavyweight champion Rocky Marciano shocked the boxing
world when on 27 April 1956 he announced his decision to retire.
The Rock was only 32 years old when he hung up his gloves and
left with a perfect 49–0 record (43 knockouts). He remains the only
heavyweight champion ever to retire with a perfect career mark.

⚜ HISTORY-MAKING KNOCKOUT ⚜

Sonny Liston made boxing history on 25 September 1962 when
he knocked out Floyd Patterson in the first round of their world
heavyweight title fight in Chicago, Illinois. Patterson was counted out
just 2 minutes and 6 seconds into the bout, making Liston the first
boxer in history to win the world heavyweight title on a first-round
KO. Liston repeated the feat against Patterson on 22 July 1963 in
Las Vegas, again knocking him out in the opening round to retain his
title. On this occasion Patterson lasted four seconds longer (2:10).

⚜ FRAZIER UNIFIES TITLE ⚜

Joe Frazier unified the world heavyweight title on 16 February 1970
when Jimmy Ellis, floored twice by Frazier in round 4 of their bout
in New York, was unable to come out for the fifth round.

✺ FIGHTING TALK (19) ✺

"I consider myself blessed. I consider you blessed. We've all been blessed with God-given talents. Mine just happens to be beating people up."
Sugar Ray Leonard

✺ FINNEGAN'S GOLD ✺

Great Britain's Chris Finnegan won the middleweight boxing gold medal at the 1968 Olympic Games in Mexico City. He beat Alexey Kiselev of the USSR on a majority decision (3–2) in the final.

✺ THE WORLD CHAMPION REBEL ✺

During the 1980s Alexis Arguello, a three-weight world champion (WBA featherweight, 1974–77; WBC super-featherweight, 1978–80; and WBC lightweight, 1981–83) briefly fought with the Contras in his native Nicaragua, but after spending a few months in the jungle he retired from the war.

✺ WE WAS ROBBED ✺

On 21 June 1932, Jack Sharkey beat the defending world heavyweight champion Max Schmeling on a controversial split decision in Long Island. After the fight, Schmeling's manager, Joe Jacobs, uttered the famous line "We was robbed" as the pair left the ring.

✺ PEP TALK ✺

On 20 November 1942, 20-year-old Willy Pep beat Chalky Wright in five rounds in New York to win the world featherweight title. The following year (19 March 1943) the former world lightweight champion, Sammy Angott, beat Pep in 10 rounds in New York to claim Pep's featherweight crown. Amazingly, it was Pep's first defeat following 62 consecutive victories.

✺ CURTAIN COMES DOWN AT THE GARDEN ✺

On 10 December 1965, Sugar Ray Robinson brought the curtain down on his illustrious boxing career when he announced his retirement from the sport at a special ceremony held at Madison Square Garden, New York.

❧ OLYMPIC GAMES' HEAVIEST HITTERS ❧

The following have won Olympic boxing gold medals in the three heaviest weight divisions (men's heavyweight since 1904, men's super-heavyweight since 1984 and women's middleweight since 2012):

Year	Boxer	Country
MEN'S HEAVYWEIGHT		
1904	Samuel Berger	USA
1908	A.L. Oldham	Great Britain
1920	Ronald Rawson	Great Britain
1924	Otto von Porat	Norway
1928	Arturo Rodriguez Jurado	Argentina
1932	Santiago Lovell	Argentina
1936	Herbert Runge	Germany
1948	Rafael Iglesias	Argentina
1952	H. Edward Sanders	USA
1956	Peter Rademacher	USA
1960	Franco De Piccolo	Italy
1964	Joe Frazier	USA
1968	George Foreman	USA
1972	Teofilo Stevenson	Cuba
1976	Teofilo Stevenson	Cuba
1980	Teofilo Stevenson	Cuba
1984	Henry Tillman	USA
1988	Ray Mercer	USA
1992	Felix Savon	Cuba
1996	Felix Savon	Cuba
2000	Felix Savon	Cuba
2004	Odlanier Solis Fonte	Cuba
2008	Rakhim Chakhkiev	Russia
2012	Oleksandr Usyk	Ukraine
MEN'S SUPER-HEAVYWEIGHT		
1984	Tyrell Biggs	USA
1988	Lennox Lewis	Canada
1992	Roberto Balado	Cuba
1996	Wladimir Klitschko	Ukraine
2000	Audley Harrison	Great Britain
2004	Alexander Povetkin	Russia
2008	Roberto Cammarelle	Italy
2012	Anthony Joshua	Great Britain
WOMEN'S MIDDLEWEIGHT		
2012	Claressa Shields	USA

❦ FRONT COVER OF *TIME* ❧

Gerry Cooney, the so-called "Great White Hope" of the 1980s, has featured on the front cover of *Time* magazine with Sylvester Stallone.

❦ FAT WILLIE CAUSES A SHOCK ❧

On 13 September 1918, "Fat Willie" Meehan caused a major sensation when he got off the canvas in round 2 to beat Jack Dempsey over four rounds. Dempsey did not lose another fight until 1926.

❦ WHEN SUGAR RAY CALLED IT A DAY ❧

After Sugar Ray Leonard lost to Terry Norris in 12 rounds in New York on 8 February 1991 for the WBC world junior-middleweight title, Leonard retired.

❦ CHAMPIONSHIP WEIGHT LIMITS ❧

Category	American	British	Metric
Straw (minimum) weight	105lb	7st 7lb	47.627kg
Light-flyweight	108lb	7st 10lb	48.988kg
Flyweight	112lb	8st	50.802kg
Super-flyweight	115lb	8st 3lb	52.163kg
Bantamweight	118lb	8st 6lb	53.524kg
Super-bantamweight	122lb	8st 10lb	55.338kg
Featherweight	126lb	9st	57.153kg
Super-featherweight	130lb	9st 4lb	58.967kg
Lightweight	135lb	9st 9lb	61.235kg
Light-welterweight	140lb	10st	63.503kg
Welterweight	147lb	10st 7lb	66.678kg
Light-middleweight	154lb	11st	69.853kg
Middleweight	160lb	11st 6lb	72.575kg
Super-middleweight	168lb	12st	76.203kg
Light-heavyweight	175lb	12st 7lb	79.379kg
Cruiserweight	190lb	13st 8lb	86.183kg
Heavyweight	any weight above cruiserweight limit		

❦ THE ELITE FIVE ❧

Five boxers managed to defeat the legendary Muhammad Ali during his professional career: Joe Frazier, Ken Norton, Leon Spinks, Larry Holmes and Trevor Berbick.

⊗ FAMOUS BOXING NICKNAMES (3) ⊗

Nickname	Boxer
Iron	Mike Tyson
The Kentucky Plumber	Marvin Hart
Jersey Joe	Joe Walcott
Lights Out	James Toney
The Living Death	Lew Jenkins
The Louisville Lip	Muhammad Ali
Macho	Hector Camacho
Madcap Maxie	Max Baer
The Magic Man	Antonio Tarver
The Manassa Mauler	Jack Dempsey
Marvelous	Marvin Hagler
The Michigan Assassin	Stanley Ketchel
The Motor City Cobra	Tommy Hearns
The Nigerian Nightmare	Samuel Peter
No Dice	Bobby Chacon
Pac-Man	Manny Pacquaio
The Pazmanian Devil	Vinny Pazienza
Porky	Dan Flynn
The President	Ike Ibeabuchi
The Quiet Man	John Ruiz
Raging Bull	Jake LaMotta
The Real Deal	Evander Holyfield
The Rock	Hasim Rahman
The Scotch Wop	Johnny Dundee
Second to	Michael Nunn
Six Heads	Andrew Lewis
Smokin' Joe	Joe Frazier
Sugar	Ray Robinson / Ray Leonard / Shane Mosley
Terrible	Tim Witherspoon
Thunder	Arturo Gatti
TNT	Tony Tubbs / Tony Tucker
The Truth	Carl Williams
The Undertaker	Harry Wills
What the Heck	Owen Beck

Did You Know That?
In the *Rocky* movies, Rocky Balboa, played by Sylvester Stallone, was nicknamed "The Italian Stallion". In *Rocky I,* Balboa fought the world champion Apollo Creed, nicknamed "The Count of Monte Fisto".

✍ THE FAB FOUR: HAGLER V. LEONARD ✌

Marvin Hagler finally met Sugar Ray Leonard on 6 April 1987 at Caesar's Palace, making the 13th defence of his middleweight crown. Leonard went into the contest having fought only once in the previous six years, and that was almost three years ago, but it did not show as the former champion deployed all his artful moves and slick punching skills in the ring against the reigning champion. The bout went the full distance, with many believing Hagler had done more than enough to retain his title, but the judges gave Leonard a controversial split decision. Hagler, too, thought that he had beaten his challenger and was stunned when the judges awarded the fight to Leonard. At no point during their bout had the champion looked to be in any form of trouble against the showboating former champion Leonard. When Leonard refused to agree to a rematch, Hagler decided it was time to hang up his gloves. To this day Hagler still feels he won.

✍ MSG IV ✌

The fourth incarnation of Madison Square Garden, in New York, opened its doors to the public on 4 March 1968. On the boxing card that night Nino Benvenuti beat Emile Griffith in 15 rounds to regain the world middleweight title, and Joe Frazier stopped Buster Mathis in 11 rounds to win New York recognition as the heavyweight champion.

✍ WHEN LAS VEGAS GOT BIG ✌

On 2 May 1955, Archie Moore the world light-heavyweight champion beat his heavyweight opponent, Nino Valdes, in 15 rounds in Las Vegas, Nevada. The bout is considered by many to be the first important fight held in Las Vegas and to mark the beginning of its rise to become the fight capital of the world.

✍ ALI'S ONLY CUT ✌

Two months after beating Floyd Patterson, Muhammad Ali was back in the ring, defending his North American Boxing Federation heavyweight title. He met world light-heavyweight champion Bob Foster in Stateline, Nevada on 21 November 1972. Despite suffering the first and only cut of his professional career, Ali pulverized Foster, who was giving away almost 3 stones (41¼ lbs), putting him down eight times before knocking him out in the eighth round.

◐ DEMPSEY AND THE WRESTLER ◑

During the 1920s, Jack Dempsey was the king of boxing, ruling the heavyweight division, while Ed "Strangler" Lewis was the king of wrestling. The public cried out for the two megastars to face one another in an exhibition match-up. Dempsey liked the idea of pitting his skills against a wrestler, and for a while the world heavyweight boxing champion trained with wrestlers to acquire the skills necessary for a wrestling fight. However, the offers on the table to face Lewis were disappointing to Dempsey, and he went off the idea. Finally, on 1 July 1940, some 12 years into his retirement as a boxer, a 45-year-old Dempsey did participate in a boxer versus wrestler match-up. Dempsey agreed to a fight under boxing rules against Clarence "Cowboy" Luttrell, a professional wrestler with no boxing background. Dempsey destroyed his challenger in just two rounds.

Did You Know That?
Dempsey also fought other famous professional wrestlers Bill Longson and Wild Bull Curry on professional wrestling shows.

◐ THE END OF TWO ERAS ◑

On the same day James "Buster" Douglas caused one of the most sensational upsets in the history of boxing when he defeated the previously undefeated Mike Tyson to become the undisputed world heavyweight champion, 11 February 1990, Nelson Mandela was released from prison after serving 27 years behind bars.

◐ THE HAT-TRICK FROM OZ ◑

Dave Sands, the reigning Australian middleweight and light-heavyweight champion, beat Alf Gallagher in 15 rounds in Sydney, on 4 September 1950, to claim the Australian heavyweight title.

◐ CHAMP HITS CHAMP ON THE FLOOR ◑

On 26 June 1922, Jack Britton retained his world welterweight title when his opponent, the reigning world lightweight champion Benny Leonard, was disqualified for hitting Britton while he was down during the 13th round of their bout in New York. Leonard's action dumbfounded everyone as it was not in his nature to be a dirty fighter, being more of a mind games boxer, and he was actually winning the fight at the time.

❧ AN IMPRESSIVE HAUL OF MEDALS ❧

The most successful amateur in boxing history may be Cuba's Master of Destruction, Teofilo Stevenson. These are his career highlights:

Olympic Games

Gold	1972 Munich	Heavyweight
Gold	1976 Montreal	Heavyweight
Gold	1980 Moscow	Heavyweight

World Amateur Championships

Gold	1974 Havana	Heavyweight
Gold	1978 Belgrade	Heavyweight
Gold	1986 Reno	Super Heavyweight

Pan American Games

Bronze	1971 Cali	Heavyweight
Gold	1975 Mexico City	Heavyweight
Gold	1979 San Juan	Heavyweight

❧ IKE THE OLYMPIAN HERO ❧

At the 1960 Olympic Games in Rome, boxer Clement "Ike" Quartey of Ghana became the first black African to win an Olympic medal when he took the silver in the light-welterweight event.

❧ FOREMAN ON THE RISE ❧

George Foreman won the 1968 Olympic Games heavyweight boxing gold medal in Mexico City. He soon turned professional and entered the 1970s with a perfect 13–0 record. Foreman's first fight against a top 10-ranked opponent was on 4 August 1970, in New York City, and he knocked out George Chuvalo of Canada in the third round.

❧ BOXING'S OLYMPIC DEBUT FIRST ❧

Boxing, dumbbells, freestyle wrestling and the decathlon all made their Olympic debut at the 1904 Games held in St Louis, USA. They were all passed at the 1901 IOC Session held in Paris.

❧ NO BEACH PARTY FOR LaMOTTA ❧

Jake LaMotta ended his boxing career on 14 April 1954 following a 10-round defeat by Billy Kilgore at Miami Beach.

⚔ FIGHTING TALK (20) ⚔

"When I was 14 years old and listening to the radio and I heard the announcer, '…and still champion of the whole world, Rocky Marciano …' I knew I wanted to be champion someday. He was a big influence in the start of my career."
Muhammad Ali, *speaking about Rocky Marciano*

⚔ BOXER TURNED ACTOR ⚔

On 2 May 1905, the world heavyweight champion James J. Jeffries announced his retirement while appearing onstage as Davy Crockett.

⚔ THE BROWN BOMBER'S BIGGEST FIGHT ⚔

On 27 March 1942, world heavyweight champion Joe Louis knocked out Abe Simon in the sixth round in New York to retain his title. It was the 21st defence of his title in just under five years, but it would be more than four years before the champion's fans would see him box competitively again. Soon after the Simon fight, Louis joined the US Army, and although he saw little in the way of active duty during the Second World War, it is estimated that he travelled more than 21,000 miles and staged almost 100 boxing exhibitions in front of approximately two million soldiers.

⚔ TYSON'S RESPECT FOR CUS D'AMATO ⚔

Mike Tyson wore black trunks in all his fights in honour of his first trainer Cus d'Amato, the man he regarded as a second father. The legendary trainer died before Tyson became the youngest ever world heavyweight champion – just as d'Amato had predicted.

⚔ BOXING'S FIRST OLYMPIC CHAMPION ⚔

At the games of the 23rd Olympiad in 688 BC the sport of boxing was introduced for the first time at an Olympics. Onomastos Smyrnaios was the inaugural Olympic boxing champion.

⚔ SWEET-TASTING BELT ⚔

Sugar Ray Robinson stopped Randy Turpin in 10 rounds in New York on 12 September 1951 to regain the world middleweight title.

🥊 21ST-CENTURY FIGHTS 🥊

19 Feb 00 The first of an enthralling trilogy of fights between two Mexican boxing legends took place in Las Vegas, with the undefeated Erik Morales taking a split decision over Marco Antonio Barreras to add the latter's WBO super-bantamweight title to his own WBC crown.

8 Jun 02 World heavyweight champion Lennox Lewis stopped the former undisputed champion Mike Tyson in round 8 to retain his crown in Memphis, Tennessee.

1 Mar 03 When Roy Jones Jr. earned a unanimous points decision over defending WBA world champion John Ruiz in Las Vegas, he made boxing history by becoming the first former world middleweight champion since 1897 to land the heavyweight crown.

18 Sep 04 Bernard Hopkins, the defending WBC, WBA and IBF champion, confirmed his status as the undisputed world middleweight champion by knocking out Oscar De La Hoya in round 9 of their contest in Las Vegas. Hopkins had not been beaten in 11 years, while it was the first time anyone stopped De La Hoya.

4 Jun 05 Ricky Hatton caused a major upset when defending champion, Kostya Tszyu failed to come out for the 12th round. He took Tszyu's IBF world light-welterweight crown before a packed home crowd in Manchester.

4 Mar 06 Joe Calzaghe outclassed the American Jeff Lacy in Manchester to claim a unanimous decision and unify the WBO and IBF world super-middleweight titles.

2 Jun 07 Shannon Briggs went into his fight in Atlantic City with Sultan Ibragimov in defence of his WBO world heavyweight championship belt. However, the younger challenger constantly laid into the champion at every opportunity and took the title from him following a unanimous points decision.

19 Apr 08 Joe Calzaghe found himself on the canvas in round 1 of his contest with Bernard Hopkins in Las Vegas but recovered to win on a split decision and extend his record to 45–0.

14 Mar 09 Amir Khan claimed a sensational fifth-round TKO win over Mexico's Marco Antonio Barrera in Manchester. Barrera suffered a cut on the forehead following a clash of heads in round 1, but the more aggressive Khan was well ahead on all three judges' scorecards.

POUND-FOR-POUND WORLD TOP 10

Rank	Boxer	Weight at last fight
1.	Román González	111½b
2.	Andre Ward	176½lb
3.	Sergey Kovalev	174½lb
4.	Gennady Golovkin	159½lb
5.	Guilllermo Rigondeaux	121¾lb
6.	Wladimir Klitschko	241½lb
7.	Terence Crawford	140lb
8.	Manny Pacquiao	146lb
9.	Shinsuke Yamanaka	117lb
10.	Kell Brook	146lb

Source: Ring Magazine, 31 October 2015

BROWN BOMBER LOSES HIS GLOVES

Not long after the legendary Joe Louis had retired from boxing, he found himself owing a large amount of money to the taxman. Louis, the former world heavyweight champion, decided to become a wrestler and wrestled from the 1950s to the early 1970s. However, in addition to making ends meet by wrestling, Louis was also used extensively as a referee for boxing prize fights.

WHEN THE BOXER FOUGHT THE MLB STAR

In 1942, Billy Conn beat future International Boxing Hall of Famer Tony Zale and had a rematch against the world heavyweight champion, Joe Louis, lined up. Conn lost to Louis in New York on 18 June 1941. However, the hugely anticipated second fight between the pair was cancelled when Conn famously broke his hand in a much-publicized fight with his father-in-law, a former professional baseball player, "Greenfield" Jimmy Smith. Following the cancellation both Conn and Louis were called up to serve their country in the Second World War, with Conn sent on a morale tour with Bob Hope and other celebrities.

Did You Know That?
Billy Conn is mentioned in the classic movie *On the Waterfront*. In the famous scene in the back of the cab, Marlon Brando playing the main character, washed-up boxer Terry Malloy, said: "I could have been a contender." In response Rod Steiger (playing Terry's brother Charley) said: "You could have been another Billy Conn."

THE KID CALLS TIME ON HIS CAREER

On 13 December 1929, Ted "Kid" Lewis fought the final bout of his 279-fight career in London and knocked out his old adversary Johnny Basham in round 3.

BOXER SEES THE LIGHT

When the heavyweight boxer Earnie Shavers retired from the sport in 1983 owing to retinal problems he became an ordained Christian minister and moved to Phoenix, Arizona where he pastored for many years. During the early 2000s he moved to England to pastor a church there.

MAGIC SPONGE DOES THE TRICK

Artie Levin hit Sugar Ray Robinson so hard in the fifth round of their bout in Cleveland, Ohio, on 6 November 1946 that after he got up off the canvas he was out on his feet. Somehow Robinson's corner-men managed to revive their man, and in round 10 he stopped Levin.

THE WINNER TAKES IT ALL

When Thomas "Hitman" Hearns annihilated reigning champion Pipino Cuevas in two rounds to win the WBA world welterweight title in his home city, Detroit, on 2 August 1980, for Hearns this was just the first of six world championships in five different weight divisions. Appropriately, when the Hearns v. Cuevas bout took place, the song "The Winner Takes It All" by Abba was No. 1 in the UK singles charts.

LAST TIME IN THE RING

On 30 December 1949, Rocky Marciano knocked out Carmine Vingo in the sixth round of their bout in New York. After the fight Vingo was so badly hurt that he was rushed to hospital and underwent brain surgery. Vingo never fought again.

CHAMP'S COMEBACK ENDED WITH KO

Jimmy McLarnin ended the comeback of the former world lightweight champion Benny Leonard on 7 October 1932, knocking him out in round 6 of their bout in New York.

❦ ROBERTO DURAN ❧

Roberto Duran, nicknamed "Hands of Stone", was born on 16 June 1951 in Guarare, Panama. The young Duran grew up in a slum area by the Panama Canal, and he left school at 13 to help support his mum, who was bringing up nine children on her own, in any way he could. He even stole fruit from an orchard owned by Carlos Eleta, who later became his manager when he turned to boxing for a living.

Aged 14 he began to fight as an amateur and after notching up 13 wins from 16 bouts he decided it was time to go professional. Roberto was ferocious in the ring, always on the front foot attacking his opponent without mercy, and after easily winning 21 fights as a professional (16 KOs) his association with Eleta began. Buying out Duran's contract with his manager for $300, Eleta hired the legendary trainers Ray Arcel and Ray Brown to fine-tune the fighter's talent. Aged 21, Roberto fought his 29th professional bout against Scotland's Ken Buchanan, the reigning WBA world lightweight champion, at Madison Square Garden, New York. Duran battered the champion relentlessly before the referee stopped the fight in round 13 to crown Duran the new world champion. Roberto was practically invincible at lightweight and went on to equal the record for lightweight defences, 12, when he knocked out Esteban De Jesus in round 12 of their contest in Las Vegas on 21 January 1978. Two years later he had to move up a division due to his increased weight, and on 20 June 1980 he took on the legendary Sugar Ray Leonard in Toronto, Canada for Leonard's WBC welterweight belt. In a memorable bout Duran won the fight on points to claim his second world championship. The much anticipated rematch, fought in New Orleans on 25 November 1980, did not live up to their thrilling first meeting and a frustrated Duran famously quit in round 8 saying *"No mas"* (No more).

On 16 June 1983, the 32-year-old Duran stopped the WBA world light-middleweight champion, Davey Moore, in round 8 of their bout in New York to claim his third different belt, but then lost to Marvelous Marvin Hagler in Las Vegas four months later. In his next fight Thomas "Hitman" Hearns laid him out on the canvas in round 2 of their WBC light-middleweight championship fight in Las Vegas. Further world title bouts followed, in which he beat Iran Barkley (winning the WBC middleweight belt on points), but lost to Sugar Ray Leonard and, in his final world championship bout, William Joppy, when the fight was stopped in round 3.

Did You Know That?
Duran had a record of 103 wins and 16 defeats in his professional career.

❧ THE SUGAR RAY ROBINSON TROPHY ☙

The Sugar Ray Robinson Trophy (formerly the Edward J. Neil Trophy) for the Fighter of the Year is awarded by the Boxing Writers' Association of America. The trophy was renamed in 2009.

1938	Jack Dempsey		Sugar Ray Leonard, Leon Spinks and Michael Spinks
1939	Bill Conn	1977	Ken Norton
1940	Henry Armstrong	1978	Larry Holmes
1941	Joe Louis	1979	Sugar Ray Leonard
1942	Sgt. Barney Ross	1980	Thomas Hearns
1943	*Boxers in all branches of the armed forces*	1981	Sugar Ray Leonard
		1982	Aaron Pryor
1944	Lt. Benny Leonard	1983	Marvin Hagler
1945	James J. Walker	1984	Thomas Hearns
1946	Tony Zale	1985	Marvin Hagler
1947	Gus Lesnevich	1986	Mike Tyson
1948	Ike Williams	1987	Julio Cesar Chavez
1949	Ezzard Charles	1988	Mike Tyson
1950	Sugar Ray Robinson	1989	Pernell Whitaker
1951	Jersey Joe Walcott	1990	Evander Holyfield
1952	Rocky Marciano	1991	James Toney
1953	Kid Gavilan	1992	Riddick Bowe
1954	Carl "Bobo" Olson	1993	Pernell Whitaker
1955	Carmen Basilio	1994	George Foreman
1956	Floyd Patterson	1995	Oscar De La Hoya
1957	Carmen Basilio	1996	Evander Holyfield
1958	Archie Moore	1997	Evander Holyfield
1959	Ingemar Johansson	1998	Shane Mosley
1960	Floyd Patterson	1999	Lennox Lewis
1961	Gene Fullmer	2000	Felix Trinidad
1962	Dick Tiger	2001	Bernard Hopkins
1963	Emile Griffith	2002	Vernon Forrest
1964	Willie Pastrano	2003	James Toney
1965	Muhammad Ali	2004	Glen Johnson
1966	Dick Tiger	2005	Ricky Hatton
1967	Carlos Ortiz	2006	Manny Pacquiao
1968	Bob Foster	2007	Floyd Mayweather Jr
1969	Joe Frazier	2008	Manny Pacquiao
1970	Ken Buchanan	2009	Manny Pacquiao
1971	Joe Frazier	2010	Sergio Gabriel Martinez
1972	Carlos Monzon	2011	Andre Ward
1973	George Foreman	2012	Nonito Donaire
1974	Muhammad Ali	2013	Floyd Mayweather Jr
1975	Muhammad Ali/Joe Frazier	2014	Terence Crawford
1976	*(US Olympic gold medal winners)* Howard Davis, Leo Randolph,		

Edward J. Neil was a sportswriter and war correspondent for the Associated Press. He died of shrapnel wounds in 1938 while reporting on the Spanish Civil War. The trophy was renamed in 2009.

❧ FIGHTING TALK (21) ☙

"The three toughest fighters I've ever been up against were Sugar Ray Robinson, Sugar Ray Robinson, and Sugar Ray Robinson. I fought Sugar so many times, I'm surprised I'm not diabetic! But I did have him off the canvas once ... when he stepped over my body to leave the ring."

Jake LaMotta

❧ BAZOOKA BATTLES ☙

In 2003 a biographical film entitled *Bazooka: The Battles of Wilfredo Gomez* was made by Cinemar Films, covering the life of the Puerto Rican boxer (nicknamed Bazooka) who won world titles at three different weights – super-bantamweight, featherweight and junior-lightweight. Gomez sold candy to earn some pocket money before becoming an amateur boxer.

❧ THE BIBLE OF BOXING ☙

The Ring magazine has been the "Bible of Boxing" since it was first published in the United States in 1922.

❧ MERCENARY BOXER ☙

At the 1956 Melbourne Olympics, Laszlo Papp from Hungary became the first boxer to win three successive gold medals at an Olympiad. The following year he turned professional but could not fight in his own country as Hungary was a Communist state and professional boxing was not permitted. Papp was forced to travel to Vienna, Austria to train and had to stage all of his fights outside the Communist regime at home. He won the European middleweight title and in 1964 he earned a shot at the world middleweight title but he was denied an exit visa because the Hungarian government resented Papp's successful by-passing of fighting professionally by staging his fights outside the country. Papp was undefeated in the ring, 27 wins and 2 draws (15 of his wins by way of knockout). In 2001 he was inducted into the International Boxing Hall of Fame.

❧ EL FEO ❧

Cuba's Luis Manuel Rodriguez, nicknamed "El Feo", was unbeaten in 36 fights before losing a split welterweight decision to Emile Griffith in a 1960 non-title fight. On 21 March 1963, Rodriguez claimed the greatest victory of his professional career when he beat Griffith to claim the world welterweight title after scoring a unanimous points decision. However, he did not have the belt round his waist for very long, losing his title to Griffith six months later on a split decision. Rodriguez was a superb boxer who possessed an extremely explosive counterpuncher and an elusive target for his opponents. Indeed, Rodriguez was trained by the legendary Angelo Dundee at Miami's 5th Street Gym, where he first met a young Cassius Clay. Clay went on to become Dundee's most famous protégé and is said to have incorporated many of Rodriguez's moves into his own fighting style. Rodriguez ended his professional career with 107 wins (49 KOs), 13 losses and 1 no contest. In 1997 he was inducted into the International Boxing Hall of Fame.

❧ FOREMAN GOES CARACAS ❧

George Foreman stopped Ken Norton in two rounds in Caracas, Venezuela, on 28 March 1974 to retain his world heavyweight title.

❧ THE ONE-EYED GYPSY ❧

Gypsy Joe Harris was a promising young boxer known for his outlandish clothes and hectic lifestyle. He drank a mixture of milk and whiskey and would often arrive at the gymnasium late for training. However, he always completed his punishing gym workouts. Harris's career was cut short after he lost to Emile Griffith in 12 rounds in Philadelphia on 6 August 1968. In the course of a routine examination two months later doctors discovered that Gypsy Joe was blind in one eye. The fighter admitted that he had contested all of his professional bouts with the disability and said that he sustained the eye injury in a street fight when he was just 11 years old. His boxing licence was immediately revoked, and after several unsuccessful appeals to be reinstated, he ended his promising professional career, aged just 22, with a record of 24 wins (8 KOs) and the solitary loss to Griffith. Harris died of cardiac arrest in 1990, aged 44, following several previous heart attacks and years of alcohol and drug abuse. Boxing historians can only guess at just how good he could have become had it not been for the blindness in one eye.

◎ WBC BELT TOSSED IN A TRASHCAN ◎

Shortly after Riddick Bowe beat Evander Holyfield on 19 November 1992 in Las Vegas, Nevada, to win the WBC world heavyweight title, Bowe chucked the WBC belt into a bin. Bowe was incensed that the WBC required him to make his first defence of his belt against their No. 1 contender, Lennox Lewis. When the champion refused to fight Lewis, the WBC made Lewis the new WBC world heavyweight champion.

◎ SCOTLAND'S BRAVEHEART ◎

Scotland's Ken Buchanan beat the defending WBA world lightweight champion Ismael Laguna in 15 rounds in San Juan, Puerto Rico, on 26 September 1970 to claim the title. The WBA and the British Boxing Board of Control (BBBC) were then in the middle of a feud, which meant that the Scot was not permitted to fight in the UK and had to fight overseas for a time. On 12 June 1971, he won the WBC world lightweight title after defeating Laguna but was stripped of the belt when he refused to defend it against Pedro Carrasco (on 18 February 1972, Mando Ramos beat Carrasco in 15 rounds in Los Angeles to win the WBC belt). Buchanan defended his WBA title a few times including a defence against Laguna on 13 September 1971, Buchanan winning in 15 rounds in New York, before laying it on the line against Roberto Duran at Madison Square Garden, New York on 26 June 1972. His bout with Duran turned out to be one of the most controversial fights in the history of boxing. After the bell had sounded to end round 13, Duran landed an illegal low punch on the champion, but amazingly the referee John LoBianco saw nothing wrong with it. When Buchanan was unable to come out for round 14, still recovering from the illegal blow and the beating he was receiving from the man nicknamed "Hands of Stone", the referee awarded the fight to the challenger by technical knockout. After the fight Buchanan had to be taken to hospital, where he underwent surgery. The brave Scot ended his career with 61 wins (27 KOs) and 8 losses. In 2000 Buchanan was inducted into the International Boxing Hall of Fame.

◎ BEHIND BUT NOT BEATEN ◎

Losing on points after the first ten rounds of his world lightweight title fight with Ray Lampkin in Panama City on 2 March 1975, defending champion Roberto Duran knocked out his opponent in round 14 to retain his belt.

◎ FIGHTING TALK (22) ◎

"Honey, I just forgot to duck."
Jack Dempsey, *speaking to his wife after he lost the world heavyweight championship*

◎ MUHAMMAD ALI – FIGHT RECORD ◎

Record: 56 wins (37 by KO), 5 defeats

Date	Opponent, venue	Result
29 Oct 1960	Tunney Hunsaker, Louisville, KY	W pts 6
27 Dec 1960	Herb Siler, Miami Beach, FL	W KO 4
17 Jan 1961	Tony Esperti, Miami Beach, FL	W KO 3
7 Feb 1961	Jim Robinson, Miami Beach, FL	W KO 1
21 Feb 1961	Donnie Fleeman, Miami Beach, FL	W KO 7
19 Apr 1961	Lamar Clark, Louisville, KY	W KO 2
26 Jun 1961	Duke Sabedong, Las Vegas, NV	W pts 10
22 Jul 1961	Alonzo Johnson, Louisville, KY	W pts 10
7 Oct 1961	Alex Miteff, Louisville, KY	W KO 6
29 Nov 1961	Willi Besmanoff, Louisville, KY	W KO 7
19 Feb 1962	Sonny Banks, New York, NY	W KO 4
28 Mar 1962	Don Warner, Miami Beach, FL	W KO 4
23 Apr 1962	George Logan, Los Angeles, CA	W KO 6
19 May 1962	Billy Daniels, New York, NY	W KO 7
20 Jul 1962	Alejandro Lavorante, Los Angeles, CA	W KO 5
15 Nov 1962	Archie Moore, Los Angeles, CA	W KO 4
24 Jan 1963	Charlie Powell, Pittsburgh, PA	W KO 3
13 Mar 1963	Doug Jones, New York, NY	W pts 10
18 Jun 1963	Henry Cooper, London, England	W KO 5
25 Feb 1964	*Sonny Liston, Miami Beach, FL	W KO 7
25 May 1966	*Sonny Liston, Lewiston, ME	W KO 1
22 Nov 1966	*Floyd Patterson, Las Vegas, NV	W KO 12
29 Mar 1966	*George Chuvalo, Toronto, Canada	W pts 15
21 May 1966	*Henry Cooper, London, England	W KO 6
6 Aug 1966	*Brian London, London, England	KO 3
10 Sep 1966	*Karl Mildenberger, Frankfurt, Germany	W KO 12
14 Nov 1966	*Cleveland Williams, Houston, TX	W KO 3
6 Feb 1967	*Ernie Terrell, Houston, TX	W pts 15
22 Mar 1967	*Zora Folley, New York, NY	W KO 7
Stripped of world championship and suspended from boxing		
†20 Jan 1970	*Rocky Marciano (movie/computer fight)*	L TKO 8
26 Oct 1970	Jerry Quarry, Atlanta, GA	W KO 3

Date	Opponent, venue	Result
7 Dec 1970	Oscar Bonavena, New York, NY	W KO 15
8 Mar 1971	*Joe Frazier, New York, NY	L pts 15
26 Jul 1971	Jimmy Ellis, Houston, TX	W KO 12
17 Nov 1971	Buster Mathis, Houston, TX	W pts 12
26 Dec 1971	Jurgen Blin, Zurich, Switzerland	W KO 7
1 Apr 1972	Mac Foster, Tokyo, Japan	W pts 15
1 May 1972	George Chuvalo, Vancouver, Canada	W pts 12
29 Jun 1972	Jerry Quarry, Las Vegas, NV	W KO 7
19 Jul 1972	Al Lewis, Dublin, Ireland	W KO 11
20 Sep 1972	Floyd Patterson, New York, NY	W KO 7
21 Nov 1972	Bob Foster, Stateline, NV	W KO 8
14 Feb 1973	Joe Bugner, Las Vegas, NV	W pts 12
31 Mar 1973	Ken Norton, San Diego, CA	L pts 12
10 Sep 1973	Ken Norton, Los Angeles, CA	W pts 12
20 Oct 1973	Rudi Lubbers, Jakarta	W pts 12
28 Jan 1974	Joe Frazier, New York, NY	W pts 12
30 Oct 1974	*George Foreman, Kinshasa, Zaire	W KO 8
24 Mar 1975	*Chuck Wepner, Cleveland, OH	W KO 15
16 May 1975	*Ron Lyle, Las Vegas, NV	W KO 11
30 Jun 1975	*Joe Bugner, Kuala Lumpur, Malaysia	W pts 15
1 Oct 1975	*Joe Frazier, Manila, Philippines	W KO 14
20 Feb 1976	*Jean Pierre Coopman, San Juan, PR	W KO 5
30 Apr 1976	*Jimmy Young, Landover, MD	W pts 15
24 May 1976	*Richard Dunn, Munich, Germany	W KO 5
28 Sep 1976	*Ken Norton, New York, NY	W pts 15
16 May 1977	*Alfredo Evangelista, Landover, MD	W pts 15
29 Sep 1977	*Earnie Shavers, New York, NY	W pts 15
15 Feb 1978	*Leon Spinks, Las Vegas, NV	L pts 15
15 Aug 1978	*Leon Spinks, New Orleans, LA	W pts 15
2 Oct 1980	*Larry Holmes, Las Vegas, NV	L KO 11
11 Dec 1981	Trevor Berbick, Nassau, Bahamas	L pts 10

* = World heavyweight title fight

† = Computer-simulated fight (see page 39)

◎ JUST CALL ME MARVELOUS ◎

The former world middleweight champion, Marvin Hagler, changed his name legally to Marvelous Marvin Hagler and starred in some television commercials, most notably for Pizza Hut and Gillette. Hagler was named *Ring Magazine* Fighter of the Year in 1983 and 1985, and in 1993 he was inducted into both the International Boxing Hall of Fame and the World Boxing Hall of Fame.

☜ LITTLE BIG MAN ☞

Canada's Tommy Burns, born Noah Brusso, was the heavyweight champion of the world from 23 February 1906 to 26 December 1908 despite the fact that he only weighed 173 lbs and stood just 5ft 7in tall. During his reign as world champion Burns, who came from an impoverished family of 13 children, defended his title 11 times.

☜ SHAKING THE KINFOLK BACK IN AFRICA ☞

Prior to turning professional, Earnie Shavers had a short but most notable career as an amateur boxer, winning the 1969 National AAU heavyweight championship. Many boxing historians regard Earnie as the hardest puncher in boxing history. Muhammad Ali fought Shavers at Madison Square Garden on 29 September 1977, and after the fight said that Shavers was the hardest puncher he ever faced: "Earnie hit me so hard, it shook my kinfolk back in Africa." Shavers finished his boxing career in 1995 with a record of 74 wins (68 by knockout, 23 inside the first round), 14 losses and 1 draw.

☜ STANDING UP FOR HIS RIGHTS ☞

In 1948 Norvel Lee, who would win the 1952 Olympic Games light-heavyweight gold medal, was arrested in his home town of Covington, Kentucky. Long before the Freedom Riders in 1961, he became one of the first blacks to sit in the all-white section on a bus.

☜ ROCK ON ☞

On 29 June 1945, welterweight Freddie Cochrane met middleweight Rocky Graziano at Madison Square Garden, New York. It was a great fight and Cochrane, despite being more than 10 lbs lighter, dominated until Graziano knocked him down late in the ninth round. Graziano charged from his corner for the final round and quickly knocked out Cochrane. At the end of the year, the contest was the first to to be named "Fight of the Year" by *Ring Magazine*.

☜ POUND FOR POUND POUNDING ☞

On 2 May 2009, at the MGM Grand in Las Vegas, Nevada, Ricky Hatton attempted to become the "Pound for Pound" champion of the world by beating Manny Pacquiao, the holder of the unofficial title. Sadly "The Hitman" from Manchester was knocked out in round 2.

❧ FIRST ABORIGINAL WORLD CHAMPION ❧

On 26 February 1968, Lionel Rose stepped into the ring against Fighting Harada as a replacement for Jesus Pimentel, who was unwell. Rose beat Harada in 15 rounds in Tokyo to claim the world bantamweight title. In doing so the 19-year-old Rose became the first Aboriginal fighter to win a world championship belt. Rose was named "Australian of the Year" in 1968, the first Aborigine to be awarded the honour. Rose retained his title on 8 March 1969, with a 15-round decision over Alan Rudkin, but then lost his belt when he was knocked out in the fifth round of his title defence against Ruben Olivares on 22 August 1969. Losses against relatively unknown fighters followed before he finally got a crack at another world title when he fought the WBC world junior-lightweight champion Yoshiaki Numata on 30 May 1971 in Hiroshima. When Rose lost a 15-round decision to Numata he announced his retirement. Later, the lure of the ring was too much for him and he made a comeback in 1975, but when he lost four of his six bouts he retired for good, ending his career with a record of 53 wins (12 KOs) and 11 losses.

Did You Know That?
In 1996 Rose presented his world championship belt to a young boy named Tjandamurra O'Shane. Six-year-old Tjandamurra had been badly burnt in a fire attack whilst playing at school in Cairns, Queensland. Rose hoped that it would speed up the boy's recovery.

❧ THE HUMAN PUNCH BAG ❧

Joe Grim, born Saverio Giannone on 14 March 1881 in Avellino, Italy, was nicknamed the "Human Punch Bag". He fought in America for 14 years and enjoyed a reputation as the man few boxers could knock out. Legends such as Bob Fitzsimmons and Jack Johnson, both hard-hitting and devastating punchers, went toe to toe with Grim but could not land a KO punch. However, despite his ability to absorb punches Grim won only very rarely. His final fight was on 22 July 1913, a sixth-round KO by Joe Borrell, and his career record was 10 wins (5 KOs), 96 defeats (6 KOs), 9 draws and 8 no decision/no contest.

❧ LOOKING THE PART ❧

In his 18-year career as a boxer the world heavyweight champion James J. "Gentleman Jim" Corbett never suffered a black eye or a bloody nose.

⚜ THE FAB FOUR: LEONARD V. HEARNS (2) ⚜

The eighth and final battle of this epic fight series took place on 12 June 1989 in Las Vegas, where Sugar Ray Leonard and Thomas Hearns went toe to toe for the WBC world super middleweight title. However, the second Leonard v. Hearns fight, which ended in a 12-round draw, was no match for their first meeting eight years earlier. Of the "Fab Four", Leonard had the best record of their eight-fight series, 4–1–1, while Hagler finished 2–0–1, Hearns 1–1–2 and Duran, the least successful, 1–0–4. Leonard ended his career with a professional record of 36 wins (25 KOs), 3 losses and 1 draw; Hagler had 62 wins (52 KOs), 3 losses and 2 draws; Hearns had 61 wins (48 KOs), 5 losses and 1 draw; and Duran had 103 wins (70 KOs), 16 losses and no draws.

⚜ THE ONE-ARMED CHAMPION ⚜

On 30 September 1904, Joe Walcott drew with Joe Gans in their 20-round world welterweight title bout in San Francisco. It was later revealed that Walcott, the defending world champion, fought many of the rounds with a broken left elbow.

⚜ AN INAUSPICIOUS DEBUT ⚜

In New York on 1 June 1904, Charley Goldman made his professional debut against Young Gardner and was knocked out in round 42 of their bout. Goldman later became famous as the trainer of Rocky Marciano.

⚜ CONN COVER ⚜

In 1995 a photograph of "Pittsburgh Kid" Billy Conn, a former world light-heavyweight champion, appeared on the cover of the British pop singer Morrissey's single "Boxers".

⚜ THE 14-YEAR-OLD PRO ⚜

At Maisons-Laffitte, near Paris, on 1 November 1908, a young French boxer named Georges Carpentier made his professional debut and beat Ed Salmon on a foul in the 13th round of their contest. Carpentier was 14 years old. On 12 February 1913, Carpentier knocked out Bandsman Rice in the second round of their fight in Paris to claim the vacant European light-heavyweight title.

⊗ FIGHTING TALK (23) ⊗

"I liked that title. I didn't want to lose it to anybody, but if I had to lose it, I'm glad I lost it to you. You're a good fighter and gonna be a great champ."
Jersey Joe Walcott, speaking to Rocky Marciano after Rocky claimed his world heavyweight belt

⊗ CERTAIN DEFEAT TURNS TO VICTORY ⊗

On 14 December 1920, the reigning world heavyweight champion, Jack Dempsey, was on the verge of losing his belt to challenger Bill Brennan in New York before the champ staged a dramatic comeback to knock out his opponent in round 12 of the contest.

⊗ UP AND DOWN ⊗

On Boxing Day 1902, Christy Williams floored Battling Nelson seven times, but in return Nelson sent Williams crashing to the canvas a staggering 42 times before finally knocking him out in round 17 of their bout in Hot Springs, Arkansas. The 49 knockdowns remains an all-time record for a single fight.

⊗ LIGHTS GO OUT IN PHILLY ⊗

On 25 July 1917, the reigning world lightweight champion Benny Leonard met the reigning world featherweight champion Johnny Kilbane in a non-title fight in Philadelphia. Leonard knocked his opponent out in the third round, the first KO suffered by Kilbane in 121 fights.

⊗ CHAMPION TOO HEAVY FOR BELT? ⊗

On 31 October 1904, Joe Gans retained his world lightweight title on a foul over Jimmy Britt after five rounds of boxing in San Francisco, California. Curiously, just one month later the champion gave up his belt, claiming that he could no longer make the weight limit.

⊗ THE OVERWEIGHT CHAMPION ⊗

On 23 April 1907 Mike "Twin" Sullivan beat Honey Mellody in 20 rounds of their world welterweight title fight in Los Angeles. Sullivan was allowed to fight despite the fact that he was over the weight limit.

✍ FIXING THE ODDS ✍

On 4 August 1947, Ike Williams knocked out Bob Montgomery in round 6 of their bout in Philadelphia to win the undisputed world lightweight title. Montgomery, Williams and Beau Jack are considered to be the greatest group of lightweight boxers to be active at one time in boxing history. Next up for Williams was a contest against former world lightweight champion, Jack. They met on 12 July 1948, and Jack was knocked out in the sixth round.

Williams was a protégé of Frank "Blinky" Palermo, the Mafia's boxing promoter, whose business partner was the former Murder Inc. button man Frankie Carbo. The authorities would not grant Carbo a licence to be a manager as he was a convicted murderer, and so he ran his fighters from his Philadelphia base through a bookmaker in New York. Carbo's stable of fighters later included world heavyweight champion, Sonny Liston. Palermo and Carbo, known as the "Czar of Boxing", would very often get one of their fighters to take a dive in a fight after they had placed large bets on their man to lose in a nominated round.

In 1940, two notorious "Murder, Inc." hit-men, Abe "Kid Twist" Reles and Allie "Tick Tock" Tannenbaum, agreed to testify against Carbo, but the case was dismissed after Reles died after falling through a window of the Half Moon Hotel in Coney Island while under police protection in November 1941. Palermo and Carbo's most notorious fix was when they ordered Jake LaMotta to take a dive against Billy Fox in New York on 14 November 1947. Some years later LaMotta admitted to having deliberately thrown the fight in exchange for an eventual shot at the world middleweight championship. Carbo and Palermo did not elude the authorities for long and they were jailed in 1961 following a successful prosecution headed by Attorney-General Robert F. Kennedy.

Did You Know That?
Reles's suicide was dramatized in the 1960 movie entitled *Murder Inc.*, with Peter Falk winning a Best Supporting Actor nomination for his portrayal of Reles.

✍ A BATTERED CHAMPION SAYS FAREWELL ✍

Emile Griffith stopped Benny "Kid" Paret in 12 rounds in New York on 24 March 1962 to regain the world welterweight title. The unfortunate Paret took such a pounding from Griffith that he had to undergo brain surgery after the fight and died nine days later.

❦ CHAMP SURVIVES PLANE CRASH ❧

On 8 January 1947, Willie Pep the reigning world featherweight champion suffered a broken leg and fractured vertebrae when the plane he was travelling on crashed in New Jersey. Less than six months later, however, on 17 June 1947, Pep was back in the ring and beat Victor Flores in 10 rounds in a non-title bout in Hartford, Connecticut. On 29 October 1948, Sandy Saddler knocked Pep out in round 4 in New York to claim Pep's world featherweight title. However, on 11 February 1949 Pep fought the best fight of his career to beat Saddler in 15 rounds in New York to regain his title.

❦ TORCH BEARER ❧

Muhammad Ali, who as Cassius Clay had won the light-heavyweight gold medal at the 1960 Olympic Games in Rome, had the honour of lighting the Olympic flame to open the 1996 Games in Atlanta.

❦ BOXING'S GREATEST TRILOGY ❧

Rocky Graziano met Tony Zale, the reigning world middleweight champion, in New York on 27 September 1946 in a fight that proved to be the first of what many believe to be the greatest trilogy in boxing history. Zale put Rocky on the floor in the opening round, but Rocky fought back and in round 2 Zale was dumped on the canvas and only saved by the bell. Rocky pounded away at Zale's body, and yet, despite the fact that he was fighting with a broken thumb, the champion sent Graziano to the floor in the sixth and watched on as Rocky was counted out. The second instalment of the trilogy was fought in Chicago on 16 July 1947, and it proved every bit as tough as the first. The champion had Rocky down early in the fight and opened up cuts around Rocky's eyes. However, with his face badly swollen Rocky fought back to stop the champ in round 6 and was crowned the new welterweight champion of the world. On 10 June 1948 they met a third time, this time in Newark, with Zale stopping Graziano in three rounds to claim back the middleweight belt.

❦ LIKE FATHER, LIKE SON ❧

When Jersey Joe Walcott knocked out Harold Johnson in round 3 of their bout in Philadelphia on 8 February 1950, he claimed a remarkable boxing double. In 1936 Walcott had knocked out Harold's father, Phil Johnson, in round 3 of their fight in the same city.

⚔ FIGHTING TALK (24) ⚔

"He can run, but he can't hide."
Joe Louis

⚔ TWO GEEZERS AT CAESAR'S ⚔

The George Foreman v. Gerry Cooney fight at Caesar's Palace, Las Vegas, on 15 January 1990, was labelled "Two Geezers at Caesar's" in reference to the claims by the boxing writers that both boxers were well past their prime. Foreman, a former world heavyweight champion, knocked out Cooney, the so-called "Great White Hope" of the 1980s, in the second round. Cooney announced his retirement from the ring after the defeat, only the third of his professional career.

Did You Know That?
Cooney was official greeter at Mr Burns' casino in the episode of *The Simpsons* entitled "Springfield (Or How I Learned to Stop Worrying and Love Legalized Gambling)". In the episode Cooney was beaten up by Ottto Man.

⚔ WATT QUITS BOXING ⚔

On 20 June 1981, Alexis Arguello beat Jim Watt in 15 rounds in London to claim the Scot's WBC world lightweight title. Two years earlier, after Roberto Duran had vacated the WBC belt, Watt fought and beat Alfredo Pitalua on 17 April 1979 to be crowned world champion, knocking him out in round 12 of their title bout. After the defeat by Arguello, Watt announced his retirement from boxing with a professional record of 38 wins (27 KOs) and 8 losses.

⚔ JESUS KO'D IN THE CITY OF ANGELS ⚔

On 1 March 1975, Bobby Chacon knocked out Jesus Estrada in round 2 of their WBC world featherweight bout in Los Angeles to retain his belt.

⚔ ALI HAS JUST LEFT THE BUILDING ⚔

On 11 December 1981, the legendary Muhammad Ali finally called time on his illustrious career after losing to Trevor Berbick in 10 rounds in Nassau.

✒ FLOYD'S FAREWELL ✒

Muhammad Ali stopped Floyd Patterson in seven rounds in New York on 20 September 1972 to retain his NABF heavyweight title in what proved to be Patterson's last fight.

✒ THE ULTIMATE BIG MAN ✒

Nikolai Valuev, born in St Petersburg, Russia, on 21 August 1973, is boxing's biggest world champion. The man who beat Evander Holyfield to retain his WBA belt in December 2008, stands 7 feet (2.13m) tall. When Valuev knocked out Clifford Etienne in a 2005 inter-continental title bout, he scaled 333lbs (23st 11lbs or 151kg) and enjoyed a weight advantage of 115½ lbs. Put into perspective, the weight limit for the light-flyweight division – boxing's fourth-lightest – is 115 lbs.

✒ SOMETHING SMELLS FISHY ✒

On 13 March 1999, the reigning IBF and WBA world heavyweight champion Evander Holyfield fought the WBC champion Lennox Lewis over 12 rounds at Madison Square Garden, New York, and the result was a draw. After the fight an investigation was carried out into how the judges scored the bout, given that Lewis totally dominated proceedings throughout. However, the result stood.

✒ ROCKY REMEMBERS ROCKY ✒

In the movie *Rocky* starring Sylvester Stallone as Rocky Balboa, Rocky's trainer Mickey told him that his boxing style and heart reminded him of Rocky Marciano. In the movie *Rocky V*, we see a flashback in which Mickey (who died in *Rocky III*) gives Rocky a necklace with a gold cufflink shaped like a boxing glove that he says was given to him by Rocky Marciano.

✒ BOXER UNDER BAZOOKA ATTACK ✒

Rafael "Bazooka" Limon stopped Idelfonso Bethelmy in 15 rounds on 11 January 1981 to win the vacant WBC world junior-lightweight title. Then, on 11 December 1982, Limon had Bobby Chacon down twice before his challenger fought back gamely to floor Bazooka in the closing seconds of the 15th and final round in Sacramento, California. Chacon took the 15-round decision to be crowned the new WBC world junior-lightweight champion.

ॐ TIGER, TIGER ॐ

On 14 December 1964, Joey Giardello beat Rubin "Hurricane" Carter in 15 rounds in Philadelphia to retain his world middleweight title. Either side of that contest Giardello fought Dick Tiger for the third and fourth time. In the third bout he won the world title by a split decision, only for Tiger to reclaim it in their fourth and final contest.

ॐ THE RISING SUN GOES DOWN ॐ

On 26 November 1953, Argentina's Pascual Perez, the 1948 Olympic champion, beat Yoshio Shirai in 15 rounds in Tokyo to win the world flyweight title. Shirai was Japan's first world champion, having won the flyweight crown on 19 May 1952 (beating Dado Marino in a 15-round decision). The loss to Perez came in his fifth defence of his belt. He fought Perez again in May 1955 and was knocked out in the fifth round. After his KO defeat by Perez he announced his retirement with a professional record of 48 wins (20 KOs), 8 losses and 2 draws. He was inducted into the *Ring Magazine* Hall of Fame in 1977.

Did You Know That?
Shirai served in the Japanese Imperial Navy during the Second World War.

ॐ UPSETTING A NUNN ॐ

James Toney caused an upset in the middleweight division on 10 May 1991 when he stopped Michael Nunn in 11 rounds in Davenport, Iowa, to win the IBF world middleweight title. Then, on 13 December 1991, Toney drew with Mike McCallum in 12 rounds in Atlantic City to retain his belt.

ॐ DICK TIGER ॐ

Dick Tiger stopped Florentino Fernandez in round 6 of their bout in Miami Beach, Florida, on 20 January 1962. Nine months later, on 23 October 1962, Tiger beat Gene Fullmer in 15 rounds in San Francisco to claim Fullmer's NBA middleweight title. In a rematch in Las Vegas on 23 February 1963, Tiger drew with Fullmer in 15 rounds to retain his belt. Fullmer and Tiger met for a third time on 10 August 1963, when Tiger stopped Fullmer in seven rounds in Ibadan, Nigeria, to claim the undisputed world middleweight title.

⟨⟨ JACK DEMPSEY ⟩⟩

William Harrison "Jack" Dempsey, nicknamed "The Manassa Mauler", was born on 24 June 1895 in Manassa, Colorado. Dempsey, one of nine children, grew up in a poor family of mixed ancestry. He fought bare-knuckle contests in saloon bars to get by and then moved across the USA living in hobo camps and working in mining and timber camps. While he was working in a shipyard he learned that one of his brothers had died, and decided to step into the ring to pay for the funeral expenses.

Dempsey earned just $3.50 for his first professional bout in 1914, and only in 1918, when Jack "Doc" Kearns became his manager, did he start making some serious money. He had tried to enlist in the US Army in the First World War, but was rejected. In 1918 he fought 21 times and lost just once, to Willie "Fat Boy" Meehan. On 4 July 1919 he met world heavyweight champion, Jess Willard, in Toledo, Ohio and won the title, battering the champion into a four-round defeat. Sadly, as Kearns had bet Dempsey's entire purse on him knocking out the champion in round 1, he never collected any money from the bout. His reign as world heavyweight champion began well with three successful defences in 10 months – against Billy Miske, Bill Brennan and Georges Carpentier, all by KO. The bout against Carpentier was boxing's first $1 million gate. Dempsey then took some time out before defeating Tommy Gibbons on points over 15 rounds in Shelby, Montana, on 4 July 1923, and then fought Luis Angel Firpo in New York on 14 September. Firpo was knocked down seven times in the opening round and was knocked out of the ring in round 2. When the ringside reporters helped Firpo back into the ring, Dempsey knocked him out.

On 23 September 1926 Gene Tunney challenged Dempsey for his heavyweight crown in pouring rain in Philadelphia. The challenger outboxed the champion over 10 rounds to take the title. A year later came the rematch in Chicago – the famous "Night of the Long Count". Dempsey floored Tunney, but the referee did not begin the count until Dempsey went to a neutral corner. Tunney got up just before the 10 count and went on to win the fight on points over 10 rounds. It was Dempsey's last fight and the fifth time he drew a $1 million gate. His final career record was: 83 fights, 62 wins, 6 losses, 9 draws and 6 no decisions.

Did You Know That?

Strangely, the boxer who Dempsey really struggled against was Willie "Fat Boy" Meehan. He won only one out of five fights against a journeyman whose career included 77 wins and 35 losses in 156 fights.

☙ FIGHTING TALK (25) ❧

"The fight is won or lost far away from witnesses – behind the lines, in the gym, and out there on the road, long before I dance under those lights."
Muhammad Ali

☙ 100 GREAT BRITISH SPORTING MOMENTS ❧

The 100 Greatest British Sporting Moments was a Channel 4 television programme which was broadcast in 2002. Viewers voted for their top 100 British and Irish sporting moments in history. The programme was presented by the former footballer turned Hollywood actor, Vinnie Jones, and five famous boxing contests were featured:

7th	Muhammad Ali v. George Foreman, the Rumble in the Jungle	1974
39th	Barry McGuigan wins the world featherweight title	1983
50th	Mike Tyson bites Evander Holyfield's ear in their rematch	1997
58th	Henry Cooper knocks down Cassius Clay at Wembley	1963
100th	Naseem Hamed beats Kevin Kelley at Madison Square Garden	1997

☙ THE CREAM ARRIVES ❧

On 31 January 1914, the future world heavyweight champion, Jersey Joe Walcott, was born Arnold Raymond Cream in Merchantville, New Jersey. Walcott later took the name of his boxing idol, Joe Walcott, the world welterweight champion from Barbados.

☙ FIREWORKS IN ATLANTIC CITY ❧

Ivan Robinson beat Arturo Gatti in 10 rounds in Atlantic City on 22 August 1998. The bout was later named the Fight of the Year.

☙ THE ROCK SUFFERS A SHOCK ❧

On 17 September 1954, Ezzard Charles split Rocky Marciano's nose, but the world heavyweight champion fought back to knock Charles out in round 8 of their bout in the Bronx, New York, to retain his title.

❧ WHEN THE LEGENDS CAME TOGETHER ❧

On 18 August 1900 a benefit fight night for the legendary former world heavyweight champion John L. Sullivan was held at Madison Square Garden, New York. The fight raised $15,000 for the 41-year-old former Champion of Champions, who was practically broke at the time, and the fans were treated to two spectacular fights featuring James J. Corbett against Bob Fitzsimmons and the then reigning world heavyweight champion, James J. Jeffries, taking on Sullivan.

Did You Know That?
Jeffries knocked out Corbett in the 23rd round of their world heavyweight scrap in Coney Island on 11 May 1900 to retain his belt.

❧ THE BAREFOOT WORLD CHAMPION ❧

On 2 May 1954, Australia's Jimmy Carruthers, the defending champion, fought Thailand's Chamren Songkitrat in the National Stadium, Bangkok, for the world bantamweight title. It was the first world championship title fight to take place in Thailand. Just hours beforehand a typhoon had hit the country, and conditions in the ring were so bad that both boxers had to remove their shoes to prevent themselves from slipping on the drenched canvas. During the fight the referee twice had to stop the fight when some spotlights exploded, causing glass to fall in the ring. Carruthers beat his challenger over 12 rounds. Two weeks after the bout, Carruthers, who was only 24, announced his retirement from boxing with a perfect 19–0 record. Six years later Carruthers came out of retirement but was not the same fighter, winning just two of the six bouts he contested.

❧ GUNBOAT SUFFERS A BROKEN NOSE ❧

On 14 March 1913, Gunboat Smith suffered a broken nose in the first round of his fight against Britain's Bombardier Billy Wells in New York. However, Smith then knocked out his opponent in round 2.

❧ BOXING'S FIRST TRIPLE CHAMPION ❧

On 25 November 1903, Bob Fitzsimmons became boxing's first ever triple champion at three different weights. Fitzsimmons beat George Gardner in 20 rounds in San Francisco to win the world light-heavyweight title, having previously claimed the middleweight and heavyweight belts.

❧ BRITAIN'S GOLDEN GLOVES ❧

Sixteen British boxers have won gold medals at the Olympic Games. Henry Mallin was the first man to retain his title and the only Briton to do so. In 2012, women's boxing entered the Olympic Games and, on 9 August 2012, flyweight Nicola Adams became the first woman ever to win a boxing gold medal, outpointing Ren Cancan of China. Here are the 17 boxing gold medals awarded to British fighters:

Boxer	Weight division	Year
Nicola Adams	Women's flyweight	2012
Luke Campbell	Bantamweight	2012
Anthony Joshua	Super-heavyweight	2012
James DeGale	Middleweight	2008
Audley Harrison	Super-heavyweight	2004
Chris Finnegan	Middleweight	1968
Dick McTaggart	Lightweight	1956
Terry Spinks	Flyweight	1956
Harold Mitchell	Light-heavyweight	1924
Henry Mallin	Middleweight	1924
Henry Mallin	Middleweight	1920
Ronald Rawson	Heavyweight	1920
Johnny Douglas	Middleweight	1908
Fred Grace	Lightweight	1908
Richard Gunn	Featherweight	1908
Albert Oldman	Heavyweight	1908
Harry Thomas	Bantamweight	1908

Did You Know That?
Johnny Douglas, the middleweight boxing gold medallist at the London 1908 Games, went on to captain England at cricket. His initials were J.W.H.T., and his reputation was as a slow-scoring batsman, so he was given the soubriquet Johnny Won't Hit Today.

❧ FIGHTING FAMILY ❧

When Ricky Hatton lost to Manny Pacquiao at Las Vegas on 2 May 2009, he was trained by Floyd Mayweather Senior, the father of the man who had ended his perfect career record in December 2007. Floyd Senior, who had trained Floyd Junior to win a world championships earlier in his career, also was a professional boxer, once losing to Sugar Ray Leonard. Two of Floyd Senior's bothers, Roger and Jeff, were world champions.

✺ BOXING GLOSSARY AND JARGON ✺

Below the belt / An illegal punch delivered below the waistband
Low blow (belt) of the opponent's trunks. The puncher can be
disqualified by the referee or have points deducted
for a low blow.

Breadbasket The boxer's stomach area, i.e. just above the belt.

Bum / Palooka A low-standard fighter – in the 1940s, many of
Joe Louis' world heavyweight title defences were
against men derided as "the bum of the month".

Clinch When a boxer holds an opponent to stop him from
throwing punches or get his own breath back.

Down / Out for When a boxer is sent to the canvas and the
the count referee gives him a count of 10.

Glass jaw / chin A boxer who has been knocked out many times is
said to have a glass jaw/chin.

Go the distance A fight, the winner of which is decided by the
judges and/or referee after the final round, is said
to go the distance. After each round, judges award
points to the boxers and the one with the most
points is the winner.

Haymaker A wild punch, an attempted knockout blow, often
thrown by a boxer who is off-balance.

Hook A dangerous punch, thrown in a powerful
downward motion to the opponent's head or body.

Jab A straight punch thrown with the leading hand,
normally straight from the shoulder. It is the most
commonly thrown punch.

Journeyman A fighter with good boxing skills but who isn't
quite at the top level. He will often be matched
against up-and-coming stars.

Kidney punch An illegal punch to the lower back or kidney region.

Kiss the canvas When a boxer has been knocked face down to the
canvas.

On the ropes A boxer who is forced to spend much of the time
defending with his back to the ropes.

Orthodox A boxer who leads with his right hand in his
normal stance.

Pulling punches A boxer who doesn't deliver his punches with his
full weight behind him. This may be because the
fight is dishonest or because the boxer does not
want to inflict unnecessary injury on an over-
matched opponent.

Punch-drunk / *On Queer Street*	*Dementia pugilistica*, a neurological disorder triggered by too many blows to the head during a career. Symptoms include: confusion, dizziness, dementia and slurred speech. Muhammad Ali's Parkinson's Syndrome is a variation of this condition.
Purse	The money offered to the boxers contesting a fight.
Rabbit punch	An illegal punch to the back of an opponent's head.
Rope-a-Dope	A tactic used by a clever, defensive boxer to tire an opponent. Standing against the ropes, he lets his opponent throw numerous punches until, when the moment is right, he will launch a counter-attack. Muhammad Ali used this tactic to beat George Foreman in Zaire in 1974's "Rumble in The Jungle".
Saved by the bell	When the bell to signal the end of a round rings with one fighter close to being knocked out, he is said to have been saved by the bell. In some fights, the referee's count stops when the bell rings.
Seconds out, round 1	Uttered by the time-keeper at the start of a bout.
Southpaw	The stance opposite to orthodox.
Sucker punch	An unexpected punch that completely catches a boxer off guard.
Sunday punch	A knockout punch.
Take a dive	When a boxer dishonestly pretends to get knocked out by a light or phantom punch, intentionally losing the fight.
Throw in the towel	When a member of a boxer's team (trainer or corner-man) feels his fighter is taking too many punches and believes his man is unable to fight on, he will throw a towel into the ring to stop – and automatically lose – the bout.
Uppercut	A powerful punch thrown in an upwards motion, often from the waist, towards the rival's chin.
Weigh-in	A pre-fight ceremony when the two boxers are checked to ensure they are within the limits for their weight class. Weigh-ins are held the day before world title fights.

⚡ DAVID V GOLIATH ⚡

The WBA World Heavyweight Championship fight between the champion, Russian Nikolay Valuev, and Great Britain's David Haye at the Nuremberg Arena, Germany, on 7 November 2009 was justifiably billed as "David v Goliath." Haye, a former unified world cruiserweight champion, at 6ft 3ins and 15 stone 5 pounds, was almost dwarfed by the mammoth seven-foot, 22 stone, 7 pounds frame of the champion. The British boxer's tactics were perfect: keeping out of Valuev's range and darting in with powerful jabs. The fight went the distance and the three judges scored the contest 114–114, 116–112 and 116–112 in Haye's favour. Haye not only became the first British world heavyweight champion title since Lennox Lewis (who retired in 2003), but also, after Evander Holyfield, only the second former world cruiserweight champion to be become world heavyweight champion too.

Did You Know That?
To put the weight disparity into some form of context, not only was David Haye the first man to successfully overcome a seven-stone weight gap, but also the WBA Minimumweight World Champion in 2015, Hekkie Budler, weighed less than five pounds (104¾ to 100) more than the difference between Haye and Valuev.

⚡ WAYNE'S COMMONWEALTH AND WORLD ⚡

Northern Ireland's Wayne McCullough won a boxing gold medal in the flyweight division of the Auckland 1990 Commonwealth Games. On 30 July 1995, McCulloch went to Nagoya in Japan and won the WBC Bantamweight Championship after beating the home-based title-holder Yasuei Yakushiji on a majority points decision. Yakushiji had made four successful defences, but after losing to McCulloch, and aged only 27, he did not return to the ring.

⚡ KLITSCHKOS IN OUTER SPACE ⚡

The Asteroid 212723 which was discovered at the Andrushivka Astronomical Observatory, in Andrushivka, Ukraine, in 2007 was named Klitschko in honour of, Vitali and Wladimir Klitschko, the world champion boxing brothers. Although both men fight or fought under the Ukraine flag, neither were born in post-Soviet Union Ukraine. Older brother Vitali was born in what is now Kyrgyzstan in 1971; Wladimir was born in what is now Kazakhstan in 1976.

❧ THE LONSDALE BELT ☙

The Lonsdale Belt is awarded to the winner of British boxing championship fights at all weights. It was introduced by Hugh Lowther, 5th Earl of Lonsdale, in 1909. If a boxer makes two successful defences of his title, he is allowed to keep the belt outright. Henry Cooper is the only boxer to win three Lonsdale Belts outright.

❧ AN IMPRESSIVE RECORD ☙

British boxer Amir Khan, a silver medalist at the Athens 2004 Olympic Games, has fought 34 times in a 10-year professional career. He has fought many of the world's best fighters and has beaten nine former world title-holders: Devon Alexander, Chris Algieri, Marco Antonio Barrera, Luis Collazo, Julio Diaz, Zab Judah, Andreas Kotelnik, Marcos Maidana and Paul Malignaggi.

❧ GRAND MASTER NO MATCH FOR PAC MAN ☙

Manny "Pac-Man" Pacquiao made a successful first defence of his WBO World Welterweight title against Joshua "The Grand Master" Clottey on 13 March 2010 at Cowboys Stadium, Arlington, Texas. Pacquiao totally dominated the fight – the first one staged at the recently opened new home of American Football Dallas Cowboys. The winning margin, as scored by the three judges, was 120–108, 119–109, 119–109. Two judges gave Clottey one round to Pacquiao's 11, but the other scored it 12–0. It was Clottey's fourth career defeat, and second in a row after losing on a split points decision to Miguel Angel Cotto for the same belt nine months earlier. It would be more than 20 months before Clottey returned to the ring, by which time he had moved up a weight to super-welterweight. In April 2014, he won the WBA International title with a unanimous verdict over Australia's Anthony Mundine.

Did You Know That?
Anthony Mundine changed careers in 2000, leaving rugby league, where he was close to international honours to take up boxing.

❧ THE ATOMIC SPIDER ☙

South Africa's Tshifhiwa "the Atomic Spider" Munyai won the vacant IBO Super Bantamweight title on a unanimous points verdict over Danilo Pena of the Philippines in Gauteng in March 2009.

⚔ BACK-TO-BACK KNOCKOUTS ⚔

On 28 August 2010, Giovani Segura (the Aztec Warrior) caused a big surprise when he knocked out the previously undefeated WBO World Light-flyweight Champion Iván Calderón in the eighth round, and in the champion's home town of Guaynabo, Puerto Rico,. Segura had been ahead on all three judges' cards when he ended the contest. *The Ring* magazine named it their Fight of the Year. Calderón got a rematch eight months later, for the same belt, but this time in Baja California, Mexico. The venue was different, but not the result, only this time the KO came midway through Round 3.

⚔ DODGY WRAPS ⚔

When "Sugar" Shane Mosley scored a ninth-round TKO of defending WBA Super World Welterweight Champion Antonio Margarito at the Staples Center, Los Angeles, California, on 24 January 2009, he felt that he had been hit too hard. Mosley was right because the California State Athletic Commission investigated the wraps used to cover Margarito's hands inside his boxing gloves. They discovered that the wraps had been coated with sulphur and calcium which, when combined with oxygen, forms plaster of Paris. Margarito was immediately suspended and returned to the ring 15 months later, fighting at Super-welterweight. He won the WBC International Super-welterweight title with a 10-round points verdict over Mexican Roberto Garcia in Aguascalientes, Mexico, in his comeback fight, but attempts to win World titles against Manny Pacquiao (WBC) and Miguel Angel Cotto (WBA Super version) both ended in failure.

⚔ TYSON IS HIS OWN MAN ⚔

Mike Tyson earned good reviews for his roles, playing himself, in *The Hangover* (2009) and its sequel, *The Hangover Part II* (2011). In the first movie, he owns a tiger which the central characters steal.

⚔ FIGHTING TALK (26) ⚔

"He is the ugliest thing I have ever seen. I have watched *Lord of the Rings* and films with strange-looking people, but for a human being to look like he does is pretty shocking."
Contender **David Haye** taunts champion Nicolay Valuev before their November 2009 WBA World Championship contest in Nuremburg, Germany

❧ SOUTHPAW ❧

The term "southpaw" is frequently used in boxing but has its origins in another sport, baseball, as a term for a left-handed pitcher. During the 1880s, baseball stadium diamonds were set out so that the batters would face east and therefore not have to stare into the afternoon sun when batting. The pitcher's left hand (or paw) would therefore be on the southern side, hence "southpaw".

❧ DIAZ LOSES FIGHT OF THE YEAR REMATCH ❧

The Ring Magazine awarded its prestigious Fight of the Year accolade for 2009 to the contest on 28 February at the Toyota Center in Houston, Texas, between Juan (Baby Bull) Diaz, the defending IBO World Lightweight Champion, and Juan Manuel (Dinamita) Marquez. Not only was Diaz's title on the line, but the vacant WBO World Lightweight Championship and WBA Super World Lightweight Championship were also at stake. Eight rounds of thrilling action had seen the judges barely able to separate the boxers, both men leading by one round on one card, and the third was all-square. In round nine Marquez launched a fierce attack and, with 20 seconds remaining, the referee awarded him the fight on a TKO. Marquez tried to end Floyd Mayweather Jr's unbeaten record, but was soundly beaten. He then had a rematch with Diaz in Las Vegas, with the WBO and WBA titles the prize. In the gambling capital of the world, Diaz was a heavy underdog, but felt his skills would see the day. Sadly for him, Marquez knew Diaz's defensive weaknesses, exploited them perfectly and won a unanimous decision.

❧ IMPRESSIVE DEBUT ACROSS THE POND ❧

Amir Khan won a silver medal at the 2004 Olympic Games in Athens. He turned professional and quickly proved himself in the paid ranks with 18 consecutive wins. Although Breidis Prescott ended with unbeaten run, Khan bounced back and became WBO World Super-lightweight Champion with a comprehensive victory over Ukraine's Andriy Kotelnik, then knocked down another Ukrainian, the previously undefeated Dmitriy Salita, three times in the first 76 seconds – the first knockdown came after 10 seconds – to retain his crown. The next challenge was on 15 May 2010, in the United States, in New York challenger Paul Malignaggi's home city at the storied Madison Square Garden. Malignaggi proved a sterner opponent, but Khan was too strong for him and won by TKO in Round 11.

⊗ HITMAN HIT FOR SIX ⊗

On 2 May 2009, Manny Pacquiao fought the reigning IBO Light Welterweight Champion, Ricky Hatton, at the MGM Grand in Las Vegas. Although it was the Filipino's first fight in the 140-pound division, "the Hitman" was no match for Pacquiao, who knocked him down twice in the opening round. The fight lasted only 129 seconds into second round, as Hatton was knocked out out cold Referee Kenny Bayliss had no need to issue a count and it took Hatton a few minutes to get back to his feet. In less than two very one-sided rounds, Pacquiao landed 73 blows, including 65 power punches; Hatton, meanwhile, landed only 18 blows, of which two were jabs. As for the blow to end the contest, *The Ring* magazine gave it the 2009 Knockout of the Year Award and named Pacquiao No. 1 in its list of the world's best pound-for-pound boxers.

Did You Know That?
In 2010, Manny Pacquiao won an election to sit in the Philippine House of Representatives and was re-elected – unopposed – in 2013.

⊗ ROYAL BATTLE FOR FLYWEIGHT CROWN ⊗

On 27 March 2010, Thailand's Pongsaklek Wonjongkam beat Koki Kameda of Japan on a majority decision in an epic battle in Tokyo to win the WBC World Championship. In fact, it was Wonjongkam's second spell as WBC Flyweight Champion, having beaten the Filipino Malcolm Tuñacao on 2 March 2001. He was an excellent and prolific champion, defending his title 17 times before losing to Japan's Daisuke Naito on 18 July 2007. The fight with Kameda was named the 2010 Flyweight fight of the year by *The Ring* magazine.

⊗ FIVE BELTS AND TWO GOLD MEDALS ⊗

At Moscow's Olympic Indoor Arena, on 5 October 2013, Wladimir Klitschko (60–3) fought Alexander Povetkin (26–0) with five belts on the line: Wladimir was the IBF, IBO, WBA (Super) and WBO Heavyweight Champion; Povetkin was WBA (Regular) Heavyweight Champion. They were also former Olympic Games Super-heavyweight Boxing gold medalists, Klitschko having won at Atlanta in 1996, Povetkin at Athens eight years later. Povetkin had no answer to "Dr Steelhammer", and although the fight went 12 rounds all three judges scored the fight 119–104, ending Povetkin's undefeated career record.

∾ BELOW THE BELT ∾

On 11 June 1930, Max Schmeling met Jack Sharkey for the world heavyweight title and won on a disqualification for a low blow.

∾ A STRANGE CAREER HIATUS ∾

Former multiple World Champion at Lightweight and Light-welterweight, Juan Diaz shocked the boxing world in June 2011 when he announced his retirement, aged 27. He had won 35 of his 39 contests (but lost four of his last six) and would surely have added to his collection of belts. Instead, he decided to enter the world of academe and studied law at Dartmouth Law School, part of the University of Massachusetts. Less than two years later, however, Diaz was back in the ring, fighting the son of former World Champion Pipino Cuevas, Gerardo Cuevas. Diaz appeared four more times, often on the undercard, but as of the end of 2014 he had won five straight contests.

∾ NOT FAST ENOUGH ∾

Wladimir Klitschko had encountered some difficulty in seeing off the challenge of American "Fast" Eddie Chambers at the Esprit Arena in Dusseldorf, Germany on 20 March 2010. However, with just seconds remaining in the final round, he caught Chambers with a left hook to the temple ending the fight there and then. The official timekeeper recorded the knockout at 2:55 of that 12th round. Klitschko thus retained WBO World Heavyweight Championship belt for the fourth time and the IBO and IBO versions for the eighth time.

Did You Know That?
Also in 2012, the Ukraine Post Office, the *Ukrposhta*, issued a set of stamps bearing the images of Wladimir and Vitali Klitschko, who represented the country with such distinction.

∾ DE GALE SETS NEW STANDARD ∾

When James DeGale won a unanimous points verdict against Andre Dirrell at the Agganis Arena in Boston, USA, on 23 May 2015 he became the first ever British boxer to win both an Olympic Games boxing gold medal and a World Championship belt. His victory at Beijing in 2008 was at Middleweight (75kg), and his IBF World Championship came at Super-middleweight, fighting at 167¼lb (76kg).

⊘ TWO EPIC CONTESTS ⊘

British Super-middleweights Carl Froch and George Groves had almost nothing in common. They were both from England, but Froch was from a small town in the north Midlands, while Groves was a brash Londoner. There was more than 10 years between the two men with 25-year-old Groves desperate to win the IBF and WBA World Championship belts held by the veteran campaigner. Froch had been in the ring with all of the greats at his weight and beaten all but American Andre Ward (his loss to Mikkel Kessler of Denmark in 2010 had been avenged three years later) whereas Groves had never tasted defeat, but he had never fought for a full World Championship belt.

The first meeting was on 23 November 2013, at the MEN Arena in Manchester. It was a magnificent contest, made so by Groves' aggression which seemed to take Froch by surprise, or the veteran had simply not prepared well for his opponent. In the first round, Groves more than got Froch's attention with a right to the head that knocked down the champion. The fight progressed with Groves scoring regular points, but he couldn't repeat that first round knockdown, and this gave Froch confidence. In the eighth round, Froch upped the tempo and Groves seemed to be unable to react. In Round 9, Groves was forced back on the ropes and Froch, scenting blood, launched a powerful array of punches. Suddenly, referee Howard Foster jumped in and waved away Froch, stopping the contest. Groves had not gone down and felt he still able to defend himself – experts disagree on whether that was true or not – and there was a huge furore. Froch, however, claimed the he knew Groves was about to be knocked out and the referee's intervention wa a good one. In truth, although Groves did lead on the judges' scorecards, two of them had only one round between them.

What the tiff only guaranteed was that there would have be Froch v Groves II, and the public clamour ensured that a much bigger venue was required. The new Wembley Stadium was chosen (the old one had been used 10 times 1924–95 – the last time when Frank Bruno beat Oliver McCall to become World Heavyweight Champion). The demand for tickets was enormous and 60,000 tickets were sold within an hour of the box-office opening. A further 20,000 were made available, making the 80,000 crowd the biggest in Britain for a boxing event since World War 2. They watched Froch give Groves much more respect and two judges had Froch leading when the fight was ended, with 17 seconds remaining in Round 8, by a stunning right which knocked Groves to the canvas. Referee Charlie Fitch did not even start the count and the Groves camp didn't argue. Froch retired early in 2015 and Groves lost another World Championship fight, to Badou Jack in September that year.

❧ 2014 COMMONWEALTH GAMES ❧

The 2014 Commonwealth Games boxing competition took place at Glasgow's Scottish Exhibition and Conference Centre. Boxers from Northern Ireland won the most medals, with nine, but England's seven comprised five gold, a silver and a bronze. These were the first Commonwealth Games to include women's boxing and, as with the Olympics two years earlier, only three weights were contested. This was the roll of honour for England, Northern Ireland, Scotland and Wales:

Boxer	Medal	Weight
ENGLAND (7)		
Scott Fitzgerald	Gold	Men's Welterweight (69kg)
Antony Fowler	Gold	Men's Middleweight (75kg)
Joseph Joyce	Gold	Men's Super-heavyweight (+91kg)
Nicola Adams	Gold	Women's Flyweight (45–51kg)
Savannah Marshall	Gold	Women's Middleweight (69–75kg)
Oais Ashfaq	Silver	Men's Bantamweight (56kg)
Samuel Maxwell	Bronze	Men's Light-welterweight (64kg)
NORTHERN IRELAND (9)		
Paddy Burns	Gold	Men's Light-flyweight (49kg)
Michael Conlan	Gold	Men's Bantamweight (56kg)
Joe Fitzpatrick	Silver	Men's Lightweight (60kg)
Michaela Walsh	Silver	Women's Flyweight (45–51kg)
Sean Duffy	Bronze	Men's Light-welterweight (64kg)
Steven Donnelly	Bronze	Men's Welterweight (69kg)
Connor Coyle	Bronze	Men's Middleweight (75kg)
Sean McGlinchy	Bronze	Men's Light-heavyweight (81kg)
Alanna Audley-Murphy	Bronze	Women's Lightweight (57–60kg)
SCOTLAND (4)		
Charlie Flynn	Gold	Men's Lightweight (60kg)
Josh Taylor	Gold	Men's Light-welterweight (64kg)
Reece McFadden	Bronze	Men's Flyweight (52kg)
Stephen Lavelle	Bronze	Men's Heavyweight (91kg)
WALES (5)		
Ashley Williams	Bronze	Men's Light-flyweight (49kg)
Sean McGoldrick	Bronze	Men's Bantamweight (56kg)
Joseph Cordina	Bronze	Men's Lightweight (60kg)
Nathan Thornley	Bronze	Men's Light-heaveyweight (81kg)
Lauren Price	Bronze	Women's Middleweight (69–75kg)

◎ REVENGE IS SWEET ◎

Italy's Patrizio Oliva won not only the Olympic Games light-welterweight gold medal at Moscow in 1980 but also the Val Barker Trophy. Oliva beat the USSR's Serik Konakbaev in the final to avenge his loss to him in the previous year's European Championships.

◎ CHASING DeGALE ◎

Both Luke Campbell and Anthony Joshua, Britain's two men's boxing gold medal-winners at the London 2012 Olympic Games are moving up the professional ladder as they aim to emulate James DeGale and add a World Championship to their Olympic glory. Super-heavyweight gold medalist Joshua won the WBC International Heavyweight Championship against Kevin Johnson in May 2015 while bantamweight winner Campbell won the WBA International Lightweight Championship against James Coyle in August 2015. Both boxers were undefeated as professionals as of the end of November 2015; Joshua was 14–0, Campbell was 12–0.

◎ GYPSY KING RULES THE WORLD ◎

On 28 November 2015, Manchester boxer Tyson Fury, "the Gypsy King", ended Wladimir Klitschko's run of nine years, seven months and six days as World Heavyweight Champion. Klitschko put his four belts on the line at the Esprit Arena in Dusseldorf, but Fury outpointed him on all three judges' cards. Fury, who had boasted that he would beat the 39-year-old Ukrainian, had a point docked in the 11th round, but still had at least three rounds in hand. The 9½-year run enjoyed by Klitschko, his 18th consecutive title defence, was two years shorter than Joe Louis's all-time record between 22 June 1937 and his retirement on 1 March 1949.

Did You Know That?
After the fight result was announced, Tyson Fury took the microphone and sang the Aerosmith hit, "I Don't Want To Miss A Thing," to his wife Paris. She had announced she was pregnant just before the fight.

◎ FIGHTING TALK (27) ◎

"Who hit me hardest? (Jack) Dempsey hit me the hardest because Dempsey hit me $211,000-worth while (Joe) Louis only hit me $36,000 worth.
Jack Sharkey, World Heavyweight Champion 1932–33

⊗ THE POCKET ROCKET ∅

As a boxer, Wayne McCullough, from Belfast, Northern Ireland, was renowned for two things: a dogged, relentless, attacking style and a cast-iron chin. The WBC World Bantamweight Champion stepped up in weight to take on two of the biggest punchers in their classes, Naseem Hamed (WBO World Featherweight Champion) and Erik Morales (WBC World Super-bantamweight Champion) and went the distance with both, although losing unanimous points decisions. Commentator Larry Merchant, covering the 22 October 1999 fight with Morales on HBO, joked, "If you look in the dictionary, under 'Tough Irishman', you'll find a picture of Wayne McCullough." McCullough was never once knocked down in his professional career.

⊗ A MAD NIGHT AT THE MGM GRAND ∅

Floyd Mayweather Jr's 42nd straight victory was certainly one of his strangest and most controversial. Victor Ortiz put his WBO Welterweight World Championship belt on the line at the MGM Grand in Las Vegas on 17 September 2011. Ortiz (with 29 wins and two draws in 33 contests) did little in the first three rounds, losing all three easily. When Mayweather caught Ortiz with a thumping shot to the head in the fourth, the Haitian-American sprang into action. He pinned Mayweather to the ropes and threw a flurry of punches which hurt Mayweather. However, for an inexplicable reason, Ortiz then head-butted Mayweather, which resulted in referee Joe Cortez deducting a point from Ortiz and allowing Mayweather time to recover. Ortiz was almost instantly apologetic as he kissed Mayweather on the cheek and, when Cortez brought the pair together to resume the contest, Ortiz hugged Mayweather. They touched gloves and Mayweather – who did nothing more than box when told to – then hit him with the sweetest of left hooks. Ortiz was dazed as Mayweather moved in for the kill, landing a right which sent him to the canvas. Vainly grabbing for the ropes trying to get back to his feet, Ortiz did not beat the count. The 22,000 fans in attendance were enraged and booed Mayweather for several minutes, then loudly cheered Ortiz.

Did You Know That?
The finish was similar to Jack Dempsey's knockout of Jack Sharkey in their world heavyweight title eliminator – the victor would face Gene Tunney – at Yankee Stadium, New York, in 1927. As the referee moved in to separate the boxers in round seven, Dempsey hit Sharkey with a left hook to the head and Sharkey was counted out.

✵ PLUS ÇA CHANGE, PLUS ÇA MÊME CHOSE ✵

Although many purists believe, with the multitude of different boxing organizations around today, that the best pound-for-pound fighter is a truer test of greatness, they remain the opinions of some or many experts. On page 133, there is the list of best pound-for-pound boxers in the eyes of *The Ring* magazine in October 2015. Six and a half years earlier, only Manny Pacquiao was on the list as chosen by *boxing.about.com* (it must be pointed out that the former list does not include Floyd Mayweather Jr., who would probably have been No. 1 had he not said he was retiring after his 12 September 2015 defeat of Andre Berto. It was Mayweather Jr's 49th consecutive win in 49 contests – and No. 48 had been a dominating victory over Pacquiao.

Rank	Boxer	Weight at last fight
1.	Manny Pacquiao	138b
2.	Floyd Mayweather Jr	147lb
3.	Joe Calzaghe	174½lb
4.	Juan Manuel Marquez	134½lb
5.	Israel Vasquez	122lb
6.	Bernard Hopkins	170lb
7.	Shane Mosley	147lb
8.	Paul Williams	157lb
9.	Rafael Marquez	126lb
10.	Miguel Angel Cotto	147lb

Source: boxing.about.com 13 May 2009

✵ IT'S A FAMILY THING ✵

The Klitschko brothers, Wladimir and Vitali, held all the major world heavyweight championship titles simultaneously for two years, five months and 13 days, 2 July 2011–15 December 2013. The only other brothers ever to be world heavyweight champions were Leon (WBA/WBC versions, 1978) and Michael Spinks (IBF version 1985–86).

✵ HOT TICKET AT WEMBLEY ✵

More than 80,000 boxing fans filled new Wembley Stadium on 31 May 2014. Top of the bill was the Carl Froch v George Groves rematch for the IBF and WBA World Super-middleweight Championship. Two British boxing Olympic champions also fought: James DeGale beat Brandon Gonzalez at super-middleweight with a fourth-round TKO, while heavyweight Anthony Joshua knocked out Matt Legg in Round 1.

THE FIRST SOUTHPAW CHAMPION

On 22 April 1994, Michael Moorer became boxing's first southpaw champion when he beat Evander Holyfield in 12 rounds in Las Vegas, Nevada, to claim the IBF and WBA world heavyweight titles.

OLYMPIC BOXING WEIGHTS

Boxing has been a part of the Summer Olympic Games since 1904, when seven men were crowned. The original weights were measured in pounds, but the change to kilogrammes came in 1948. There has been constant change in the weight classes and the number. At London 2012, when women's boxing was first contested, there were 10 classes for men and three for women. These were the weight classes (to the nearest lb):

Category	Kilogrammes	Lbs	St/Lb
MEN'S			
Light-flyweight	46–49	101–108	7st3lb–7st10lb
Flyweight	49–52	108–115	7st10lb–8st3lb
Bantamweight	52–56	115–123	8st3lb–8st11lb
Lightweight	56–60	123–132	8st11lb–9st4lb
Light-welterweight	60–64	132–141	9st4lb–10st1lb
Welterweightt	64–69	141–152	10st1lb–10st12lb
Middleweight	69–75	152–165	10st12lb–11st11lb
Light-heavyweight	75–81	165–179	11st11lb–12st11lb
Heavyweight	81–91	179–201	12st11lb–14st5lb
Super-heavyweight	91 and over	201 and over	14st5lb and over
WOMEN'S			
Flyweight	48–51	106–112	7st8lb–8st0lb
Lightweight	57–60	126–132	9st0lb–9st6lb
Middleweight	69–75	152–165	10st12lb–11st11lb

Did You Know That?
Although the limits have changed for all weights, except for the 91kg minimum for Super-heavyweights, there are two weight classes no longer contested, Featherweight and Light-middleweight.

CELEBRATING THE GREATEST

In Louisville, Kentucky, his birthplace, the Muhammad Ali Center is a museum and cultural centre celebrating "The Greatest's" life.

℘ MAYWEATHER MATCHES MARCIANO ℘

Floyd Mayweather Jr does not win beauty contests, but he does win boxing contests – and like no other champion since the days of Rocky Marciano. "Money", as he is known, announced in the summer of 2015, that his contest against Andre Berto for his WBA Super and WBC World Welterweight Championship belts at the MGM Grand in Las Vegas, Nevada, on 12 September 2015, would be his final one. Assuming, he stays retired, Mayweather Jr finished his career with the same 49–0 record achieved by Marciano in the 1940s and 50s. The similarity ends there. Without doubt, Mayweather Jr would be in any argument about the greatest defensive boxers of all time; "the Brockton Blockbuster" was known for his knockout power. Marciano would never have been called "Pretty Boy" – another Mayweather Jr nickname – given his propensity for bleeding. Maybe that is why Marciano didn't let his fights go the distance very often. In fact 88 percent of his fights (43 of them) ended early; a very different story to that of Mayweather Jr, who needed judges' verdicts 23 times out of 49 professional contests. On average a Mayweather Jr fight lasted eight rounds; with Marciano the average was round five.

℘ FIGHTING TALK (28) ℘

"I can fight anybody, it will depend on my promoters. I'm just a fighter, doing my job, training and keeping at 100 percent."
Manny Pacquiao, after his second-round knockout of Ricky Hatton for the IBF World Light-welterweight Championship on 9 May 2009.

℘ SHORT BUT NOT SWEET ℘

Texan Lou Savarese and New Yorker Mike Tyson fought at Hampden Park, Glasgow, Scotland on 24 June 2000. The contest lasted 38 seconds, which was eight seconds longer than Marvis Frazier – Joe's son – managed against Tyson in Glen Falls, New York, in 1986.

℘ SMOKIN' NO MORE ℘

The boxing world was in mourning after it was announced that Joe Frazier had died on 7 November 2011, at the age of 67. Most famous for his three epic fights with Muhammad Ali in 1971, 1974 and 1975 (the Thrilla in Manila), he was WBC and WBA World Heavyweight Champion between beating Jimmy Ellis in February 1970 and being blasted out in two rounds by George Foreman in January 1973.

✑ INDEX ✑

ABOUT THE AUTHOR

John White's love affair with boxing began 45 years ago, in March 1971, when Muhammad Ali and Joe Frazier met for the first time. He watched the fight live and has avidly followed the sport ever since. An Irishman, from Belfast, he has watched and celebrated as many of his countrymen, Dave McAuley Barry McGuigan and Steve Collins, to name but three, became world champions. An inveterate researcher, John has built up an astounding database of facts, stats and stories across the wide world of sports and he has put it to good use with his series of *Miscellany* titles. The sports to have enjoyed his unique insight are: Boxing, Football, Rugby Union, Cricket, Golf, Horse Racing, Formula One, MotoGP and Cycling. These are the other titles in the series:

The England Football Miscellany
The Manchester United Miscellany
The Liverpool FC Miscellany
The Celtic Football Miscellany
The Rangers Football Miscellany
The Premier League Football Miscellany
The Six Nations Miscellany
The Cricket Miscellany
The Golf Miscellany
The Tour de France Miscellany
The Horse Racing Miscellany
The Formula One Miscellany
The Moto GP Miscellany
The Olympic Games Miscellany